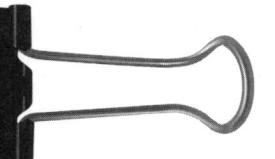

D1359410

Love
Mom & Larry

The Ultimate
Office
PRANK BOOK

DISCLAIMER: I take no responsibility [...] nployment, legal, or romantic status as a result of perpetrating any prank herein. Face it, some o[...] you in Big Trouble with the Boss, maybe even lead you to a cushy bench in the Big House. But rest a[...] you with some helpful phone numbers, just in case you get to make that one phone call. Let me repe[...] se pranks will certainly get you fired and some will get you in BIG legal trouble. Others are just plain dang[...] w are really gross. So prank at your own discretion and at your own risk. But do Prank On, dude!

~~Mac B. Fired~~

DISCLAIMER:
Mae B. Fired and the publisher officially take no responsibility whatsoever for your employment, legal, or romantic status as a result of perpetrating any prank herein. Face it, some of these escapades WILL get you in Deep Trouble with the boss, and may even lead you to a cushy bench in the Big House. But you can rely on the helpful phone numbers provided here in case you have an opportunity to make that one phone call.

We repeat: Some of these pranks will certainly get you fired and some will get you into serious legal trouble. Others are just plain dangerous. And a few are really gross. So engage in these antics at your own discretion and at your own risk.

Happy hijinks!

Published by
Adams Media, a division of F+W Media, Inc.
57 Littlefield Street, Avon, MA 02322. U.S.A.
www.adamsmedia.com

ISBN 10: 1-59869-996-2
ISBN 13: 978-1-59869-996-8

Printed in the United States of America.

J I H G F E D C B A

Library of Congress Cataloging-in-Publication Data
is available from the publisher.

This publication is designed to provide accurate and authoritative information with regard to the subject matter covered. It is sold with the understanding that the publisher is not engaged in rendering legal, accounting, or other professional advice. If legal advice or other expert assistance is required, the services of a competent professional person should be sought.

—From a *Declaration of Principles* jointly adopted by a Committee of the American Bar Association and a Committee of Publishers and Associations

Many of the designations used by manufacturers and sellers to distinguish their product are claimed as trademarks. Where those designations appear in this book and Adams Media was aware of a trademark claim, the designations have been printed with initial capital letters.

Interior illustration by Elisabeth Lariviere
paperclip by Elisabeth Lariviere
pins: © iStockphoto/Simfo

This book is available at quantity discounts for bulk purchases.
For information, please call 1-800-289-0963.

Contents

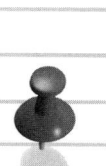

Pranks for those new to the game.

Moving up in the world means paying your dues.

Congratulations—you've been promoted!

I actually died the folley chair. Wheww... was that guy mad!

Only top-level executives are ready for these
sneaky stunts.

Welcome to the Jungle— the Office Jungle

It's a jungle out there, and in the office— as in any tribe—it's every man for himself.

Let me guess, you're having one of THOSE days. **Kisses the Boss's Ass** just pointed out your big mistake to **Idiot with All the Power** and explained how he fixed everything. **Sleeps Her Way to the Top** received the promotion you've been working toward for three years, and to make matters worse, **Stick Up Her Butt** keeps nagging you about an expense report that's off by 29 cents. After a day like today, which seems like every other day in this drab Cubicleland they call an office, you're starting to think **Naps at His Desk** has the right idea. After all, if **Clueless** still has a job, then surely you can't lose yours.

So why not liven things up? Exact some revenge and have something to look forward to every day. Yes, that's right, play some pranks.

Don't worry, you can test the waters before diving in. You shouldn't expect perfection the first time out. Try a whoopie cushion first or maybe a dribble glass. But I promise you, once you get started you're not going to want to stop. It won't be long before you stop worrying about your next performance review and move well beyond those pranks. Each prank has been rated with an appropriate risk level so you can start out light with pranks that will only earn you an **Eye Roll** or **Summons from the Boss**. Give a few a try and you're going to feel the need to ratchet up the risk level and chance a prank rated **Note in Your File**, or throw caution to the wind and pull a prank rated **Pink Slip** or **Lawsuit!**

Lawsuit	Most Risky
Pink Slip	
Note in Your File	
Summons from the Boss	
Eye Roll	Least Risky

Who knows? Maybe your position as **Office Clown** will breathe new life into your dead-end job or at the very least your reputation. The best part is that it doesn't necessarily require overtime. The level of effort is optional, of course. And so is the amount of preparation.

But remember:

A good prankster will always have a secret camera in place to record reactions and share them with the world. (How else do you think you're going to get famous on YouTube?) The first section of **Entry-Level** jokes are easy to execute. Even **Old Timer** could get the job done. More ambitious pranksters will want to jump right up to **Middle Management**. But if you want to make it to **Executive Level**, you're going to have to put in some extra hours at the office. Outsmart **Idiot with All the Power**. Wipe that smile off of **He Who Knows Everything's** face. Catch **Sleeps Her Way to the Top** with her pants down. Have fun, dude! And I'll see YOU in the unemployment line!

P.S: Every time you see a sticky with "**CYA**" on it, you'll have a quick excuse to **cover your ass**! (These will definitely come in handy.)

Company Directory

Every company has one, it's where you turn to for phone numbers, titles, and personal tidbits about your fellow workers. Since this is also your most valuable source for identifying victims, I recommend you keep it close by at all times.

COMPANY DIRECTORY

Name	Extension	Department	Known For
Caffeine Freak	122	Sales	His Starbucks triple venti extra-shot skim mocha addiction.
Clock Watcher	530	Accounting	Turning into the Invisible Man at five o'clock.
Clueless	000	Reception	Her overenthusiastic use of the word: "Awesome!"
Conspiracy Theorist	666	Publicity	His overflowing bookcase, full of evidence for a case against the company for bugging his office.
Forever an Assistant	222	The Boss	Her eagerness to brew coffee, file useless paperwork, and take phone messages for the Big Boss Man.
He Who Knows Everything	112	Executive	Waxing poetically on any topic, including proper coffee brewing and filing techniques.
Hot Temp	None	Everywhere	Nothing. Who is she again?
Idiot with All the Power	#1	Me	Thinking he's fooling us by being so chummy. (Joke's on him!)
Kisses the Boss's Ass	113	Wherever the boss needs me	Recently getting caught sketching ideas for her "I heart Big Boss Man" tattoo.
Mooch	567	Accounting	Sneaking into the fridge and stealing your lunch.
Mr. Competitive	123	Sales	His bigger, better, bolder—and more annoying—attitude on everything.
Naps at His Desk	Phone is off the hook	Customer Service	Loud snoring and the wet spot he leaves on his desk after peeling his face off his papers at the end of the day.

Name	Extension	Department	Known For
Nervous Nelly	888	HR	Her standing lunch date with Pansy and Sally.
Office Narc	999	HR	His volunteer work with the police and fire squad and for sometimes wearing his "badge" to work.
Old Timer	1000	Sales	Humming Springsteen's Glory Days while smoking in his office.
Sleeps Her Way to the Top	798	Sales	Her "power" suits and need to please…er, I mean succeed.
Stick Up Her Butt	345	Accounting	Redefining anal retentiveness.
Super Slob	076	Marketing	His stinking black hole of a cube.
Talks Too Much	703	Publicity	Calling in sick due to chronic verbal diarrhea.
The Hypochondriac	402	Accounting	The hand sanitizer on her desk and that time she brought her own dishes to the company BBQ.
Woeful Wallflower	938	Reception	The "family" pics featuring her cats: Fluffy, Marmalade, Cuddles, Boo Boo, and Petey.

 Add your own

Accomplice Questionnaire

Every good prankster needs an accomplice or two, those people who can stand by your side when the chips are down and the stunts are big. Choosing an accomplice is hiring an assistant of the highest sort. Not just anyone can do this job. It has to be someone stealthy, crazy, and willing to take a fall.

With that in mind, I've created a questionnaire that should be used before revealing your master plan. By using proper interview techniques I guarantee you'll find a teammate who is strong, brave, and won't throw you under the bus.

PRANKSTER PREQUALIFIER

1. Which would be your code name of choice?

a. Papa Bear

b. Running Scared

c. The Narc

d. No Fear

2. Where do you see yourself in ten years?

a. Working the drive-thru at Wendy's.

b. Mastering the art of Kung-Fu.

c. In the basement, playing Guitar Hero.

d. Running this place.

3. What would be your weapon of choice?

a. Staple gun

b. Laser pointer

c. Stun gun

d. German short-haired pointer

4. Do you currently own any of the following?

a. Power tools

b. Jello molds

c. Super glue

d. Black ski mask

5. What is your favorite movie?

a. The Italian Job

b. Caddyshack

c. Office Space

d. Pretty Woman

6. How much do you value your job?

a. Get me the f*&$% out of here!

b. It's a living.

c. It's hardly a job.

d. It's a dream come true.

7. Describe your arrest record:

a. Arrest record? Only crooks have those.

b. Unpaid parking tickets here and there.

c. Does smoking pot count?

d. Felony charges, but I didn't do it.

8. What are your motivations for becoming an accomplice in pranking?

a. I'm bored.

b. It's time to get back at all of those idiots we work with.

c. I thought this was an interview for Fire Warden?

d. I want to be just like you.

9. When faced with a bust what is your first reaction?

a. RUN!

b. Talk my way out of it.

c. Point to the guy next to me.

d. Curl up in a ball and pee my pants.

10. Your impression of the boss is:

a. He's the best friend I've ever had.

b. He's my mentor.

c. He's a loser.

d. He's sexy.

Now take a close look at the answers your potential accomplice has given. Obviously there's no real right or wrong here since, logically, this whole thing is just plain wrong. Unless you're very, very lucky, there is no such thing as a universal accomplice. What one person might pull off with finesse, another might screw up miserably.

So look at the answers you've been given and think about the specifics of the job. If you only have one response of Jell-O mold ownership, you're probably going to need to use him at one point or another, but he might not be the right guy for when power tools are needed. Check out the following page for some more insight on those A, B, C, and D answers.

Did your accomplice answer primarily A's?

If so, he's probably not the man for any of your jobs. In fact, he might be the best victim you've got. He's sensitive, weak, and possibly a narc. He's not the kind of man you'd want on your team.

An interviewee who answered mostly B's is getting closer . . .

This guy's probably not ready for middle management and certainly not executive material. He's got some good ideas and really wants to make this work, but he's soft and can easily be broken. Proceed with caution with a B-level accomplice by your side.

And then we come to C's.

This guy might very well be the closest thing you have to a Robin for your Batman. He's crafty, sneaky, and wants to wreak havoc in the office. A warning though, he's also ambitious and you'll need to be careful about where his ambitions and loyalties lie. If he's thinking promotion, your relationship could quickly crumble.

One might think an accomplice who answers D's is the man for the job.

He's brave, strong, and probably even good looking. The problem? He wants to be the boss, and I mean that literally as well as figuratively. (Have you ever noticed how the Big Bossman wears a pink tie on Wednesday and your guy wears an identical tie on Thursday?) Be wary of anyone who answers mostly with D's; he could be ratting you out at this very moment.

Entry-Level Pranks

Pranks for those new to the game

If you're an office-prank virgin, I advise you to start slowly. Whether you're the guy who stuck it out in the mailroom for twenty years, waiting for someone to remember your name, or you're the new kid on the block, don't worry. You're ready for this. Once you're in the groove, you'll forget what your office life was like prepranking! When in doubt, REMEMBER, even **Idiot with All the Power** could handle this stuff.

Er, Excuse Me?

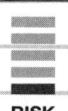

TARGET: Naps at His Desk

RISK LEVEL

Office Supplies

Computer

This is a super fun prank for everyone involved, especially those seated around **Naps at His Desk**. When Naps is away (on an important meeting in the lounge with Mr. Couch) slip into his seat and change his sound settings. Add a fart when he opens his e-mail or a burp when an e-mail is sent. Make horns honk when he gets new mail and dogs bark when he deletes a file. Whatever you do, make sure the volume is up and loud so that everyone can hear.

CYA

Blame it on the IT Department!

Singing in the Rain

RISK LEVEL

TARGET: Stick Up Her Butt or anyone with an aversion to messiness

Office Supplies

Umbrella, confetti

What a fun idea for **Stick Up Her Butt**, the perfect prank for the perfect pain. She's always perfectly coiffed, perfectly poised, and perfectly in control. She would never show up on a rainy day without an umbrella or unprepared for a meeting. So what better way to shake her perfect world than by adding a little confetti?

While **Stick Up Her Butt** is off attending one of her perfectly planned meetings, you sneak into her office and dump as much confetti as you can into her umbrella. Make sure it's small, and make sure it's paper. You know . . . the kind that will stick to her hair and fall into her clothes. The good kind.

Now all you have to do is wait for her to leave. Maybe you'll even be extra timely yourself and walk out of the building with her. Watch the rain come down when she raises that Mary Poppins showpiece up over her head and flings it open. Just remember to stand back so you don't get hit!

Ransom Notes

RISK LEVEL

TARGET: Mr. Competitive (or anyone with a passion for collecting)

Office Supplies

Paper, prized desk possession

Every office has a guy who insists on covering his desk and wall space with goofy collectibles. In this office, it just so happens that **Mr. Competitive** has his prized sports-freak bobblehead collection, which he is convinced will be worth something someday. Three words come to mind when thinking of collections of this ilk: annoying, embarrassing, and (most of all) stupid.

Well finally, on one of those cold, rainy, quiet office days, you have an opportunity to liven things up. Once you've settled in to your own cubicle with your Starbucks venti-vanilla-soy-double-shot-latte it's time to make a plan. Your first step is to plot out the scavenger hunt, and for that you'll need a creative accomplice. She's the one with all the fun ideas and the one who isn't afraid to think outside of the box.

Once the two of you have settled in, start planning the hunt, because before you raise suspicion by taking a coveted item you need to have a plan. For those who have lived life without a scavenger hunt, those who have also apparently lived in a hole somewhere, you need to leave clues at each so-called hiding place. Clues that send your victim off and running to the next possible location.

The first clue can be left on **Mr. Competitive's** desk and for maximum fun should probably be a ransom note. Something along the lines of, "I have Mr. Bubbles and for a small price he can be yours again. Take this lead and search for him behind the caffeine machine." This will obviously lead your victim to the coffee maker where you've left yet another clue.

Allow your imagination to run and don't be afraid to lead **Mr. Competitive** far and wide—after all, he's going to want to win his prize back! Take him from office to office; floor to floor; and even outside to the hot dog stand, parking lot, and

that weird tree that the office smokers always hide behind. Let the hunt go for as long as your clues can be clever, but also keep an eye on the clock, because while your victim may love his toys he's also not going to search all day for them.

And don't forget to actually leave Mr. Bubbles at the last hiding place, because a scavenger hunt is no fun unless there's actually a prize at the end.

Fast-Track

Put Mr. Bubbles on eBay for $1. (Be sure to e-mail the link to Mr. Competitive from an anonymous address!)

Time to Make the Donuts

RISK LEVEL

TARGET: Kisses the Boss's Ass

Office Supplies

None

Tell **Kisses the Boss's Ass** the head honcho wants her to order a load of donuts for an important executive meeting (that she's not invited to) and take them into the conference room in the middle of the meeting. Watch her walk in with a large tray of donuts. This is worth telling others about so you can enjoy the scene together. Besides, there will be all those donuts to eat . . .

Prank Pitfall

Make sure to let her know once the boss is out of the office, since she's likely to double check with him (that brown-noser!)

Name That Tune!

TARGET: Woeful Wallflower

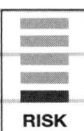

Office Supplies

None

Enlist the help of office-mates who attend the same meetings as you do. When you get to the conference room, sit next to **Woeful Wallflower**. Once the meeting is underway, hum a nonstop, stirring rendition of "It's a Small World, After All" off and on throughout the duration of the meeting. When your boss asks who's doing it, persuade your fellow office pranksters to all look over at your unsuspecting victim.

It's a small world...

A Standing O!

RISK LEVEL

TARGET: Kisses the Boss's Ass

Office Supplies

Powerstrip, The Clapper

Could there possibly be a better pranking gadget than The Clapper? So many fun things you can do with this clever creation.

Almost everyone who works in an office works off a power strip. Because most offices have one outlet for every fifteen pieces of electrical equipment, they are as essential as your computer. And of course **Kisses the Boss's Ass** uses his to plug in his radio (which is annoyingly tuned to know-it-all shock jocks 24-7). Note that this prank is especially fun and effective if you sit

right next to **Kisses the Boss's Ass**. That way you can put in as little effort as possible.

About two weeks before the Main Event, you need to take up clapping. It goes something like this: Make a joke, clap for yourself. Clap to get the **Hot Temp's** attention and clap when someone else does something wonderful, stupid, or just walks by. Make it a regular part of your routine. The bonus of this is that you're going to annoy people before the prank even begins!

Once you've made it very clear that you are now a

"clapper," that clapping is as much a part of you as, well, lips on bum-cheeks is to **Kisses the Boss's Ass,** you're ready to go.

When **Kisses the Boss's Ass** is away from his desk get in there and surreptitiously attach The Clapper® to either his entire power strip or just the radio plug. Whichever you choose, make sure it's something that will turn on each time the power comes on, and off when it goes off. (Note that a computer might not work in this instance.) Once **Kisses the Boss's Ass** sits down to listen to his favorite daytime DJ, you can start clapping—it is funny after all—and watch his frustration. It's going to make you want to applaud even more . . .

Sweat Equity

This requires more effort and resources than the average prank, but you can get a clapper for less than a 20-spot, and the payoff makes it more than worth it. Clap on!

Speak Clearly, Please

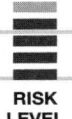

RISK LEVEL

TARGET: Sleeps Her Way to the Top

Office Supplies
Baby monitor

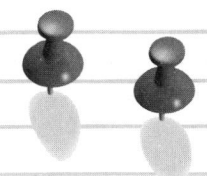

For this prank you'll need to get your mitts on a baby monitor. Borrow one from a friend or maybe an accomplice will come through for you. Hide the microphone in **Sleeps Her Way to the Top's** office.

Then find a safe, hidden spot for the speaker device in the office restroom or better yet, in the break room. You might end up on the unemployment line for this one, but your legendary status as Prank Royalty will long outlive your Welfare stint.

#Easy Marks

Also consider pranking on Kisses the Boss's Ass, Conspiracy Theorist, or Idiot with All the Power.

The Corner Office Goes To ...

RISK LEVEL

TARGETS: Forever an Assistant or Idiot with All the Power

Office Supplies

Nameplates

One day after work, when you've stayed late to burn the midnight oil (yeah, right) have a little fun. Take five minutes to switch all the nameplates around. Give **Forever an Assistant** the coveted corner office and move **Idiot with All the Power** over to a tiny cube. Depending on the crew you work with, this is a prank that could take days to discover and might be especially fun if you have extra special visitors coming in for an office tour.

Faux Fiesta

TARGET: Mr. Competitive

RISK LEVEL

Office Supplies

Letterhead

Memos are the bane of every office worker's existence. Do we really need a memo to tell us the copier is broken? Isn't it obvious when you walk in the room and the repairman's butt is sticking high into the air? Well, here's your chance to have a little memo-fun. Make those annoying notes work for YOU for a change . . .

This is the perfect prank for **Mr. Competitive**. The guy who always does it one better and two bigger. Remember to deliver his memo the day before the "party" and make sure it's scheduled during one of the boss's big meetings. Personalize and send the following:

Fast-track

Add an imaginary charity to the mix, and collect money to put toward your next elaborate prank!

To: All Employees
From: The Big Boss Man
Date: Tomorrow, 3 P.M.
Re: A Costume Party!

In special appreciation of all the hard work you do we're hosting the first annual Employee Appreciation Costume Party. First prize for best costume is an extra week of vacation time.

Rules:

1. Bring your costume to work, but keep it hidden. Secrecy is imperative since the stakes are high.
2. At 2:45, sneak away to dress for the party.
3. 3:00 is the big reveal. Head straight to the conference room for the big event.

Attendance is mandatory.

My Ears Are Ringing

TARGET: Talks Too Much

RISK LEVEL

Office Supplies

Phone, tape

Aren't you sick of **Talks Too Much** and her constant babble? Is it really necessary to be on the phone all day long? And don't her ears hurt? Well here's a prank that might actually give you five minutes of peace and quiet.

While **Talks Too Much** is away from her desk, slip a piece of scotch tape over the receiver button on her phone. When the phone rings and she goes to answer it the ringing won't stop, and it will take her at least a phone call or two to figure out the problem.

Fast-track

Frustrate her even more by calling all morning!

Fishing for Suckers

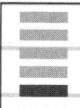

RISK LEVEL

TARGET: Clueless

Office supplies

Phone, fishing line

This is an easy prank anyone can do, but that doesn't make it any less fun. Before the day begins, slip into **Clueless's** seat and using fishing line tie the phone cord together as close to the base as possible. The minute he makes a grab for the phone, watch the entire system go flying off his desk.

A Paper Trail

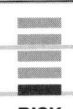

RISK LEVEL

TARGET: Anyone and everyone

Office Supplies

Copy machine

The next time you're sent to the copier to photocopy yet another report, take a moment for some fun. In the days before computers this was really where all office hijinks happened, but alas, times have changed and the fun has moved elsewhere. That doesn't mean that you can't still do some damage here.

Before leaving the room, your copies safely in hand, reset the copier to print 100 copies at low resolution. Since few people actually look at the machine before pressing Start, their panic will ensue when the machine won't stop.

COPY MACHINE

Crazy Copies

RISK LEVEL

TARGET: Anyone in the right place at the right time

Office Supplies

Paper, a paperclip, copier

Slip into the copy room with a plain white sheet of paper, paperclip attached. And get copying. I would advise a hundred or so copies. Let that machine run. Once you have all of your copies in hand slip them back into the paper tray, making sure that the picture of the paperclip is going to be on the printed side of the page when it comes back out again. The confusion this prank causes is truly amazing. The same, very bright person, will pull her copy out of the machine three or four times to check for the paper-clip, while others will assume a paperclip is stuck in the machine and call the repairman.

Duration

Do this for a week straight, or once a week for a month, using a different office supply each time.

Mickey Mouse

RISK LEVEL

TARGET: Old Timer

Office Supplies

One Post-it note or tape, mouse

When **Old Timer** is away the mice will, well . . .
stop playing in this case.

To successfully complete this prank you'll first need to know what kind of mouse **Old Timer** is using. If it's a rollerball mouse (the kind with a little ball at the bottom), you're going to need tape. And if it's an optical-light mouse (the kind with a light on the bottom), you'll need a Post-it note.

Once **Old Timer** steps away from his desk, and you won't need a lot of time, slip over and either tape or Post-it his mouse.

Make sure you cover the ball or light. Give him no more than five minutes before panic ensues and IT is called.

CYA

Blame that lunatic in IT again. (Best if this is delivered by Consipracy Theorist.)

Monitoring the Fun

RISK LEVEL

TARGET: Idiot with All the Power

Office Supplies

Computer

This simple little prank is easy and fun, and can always cause quite a stir. When **Idiot with All the Power** steps away from his desk for a little vending machine treat, which he does daily at 3:17 P.M., slip in and adjust the settings on his monitor so you get nothing but a plain, black screen. When he returns, Snickers bar in hand, he's sure to panic. After all, **Idiot with All the Power** can barely turn on the machine, let alone diagnose a problem. It won't be but a matter of seconds before IT is coming up to suss out how **Idiot's** computer could have died during a short, fifteen-minute break.

Chain Reaction

RISK LEVEL

TARGET: Sleeps Her Way to the Top

Office Supplies

None

There's nothing **Sleeps Her Way to the Top** loves more than a gift, especially if it's shiny and new, something she can wear and show off to all of her friends. Isn't it time that you chipped in and gave her a gift too? While **Sleeps Her Way to the Top** is away primping in the bathroom or maybe at "lunch" with the boss you can slip in and spend some time with her paperclip container. String all the paperclips into one big long chain and put them back into place. Imagine her frustration, or maybe her joy, when she goes to pull one out only to find they are all attached into a beautiful necklace.

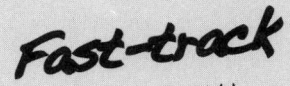

Fast-track

Pour something gross and gooey in her paperclip container.

WIDGET/TEX PERSONNEL FILE
PERSONAL AND CONFIDENTIAL

Date: *December 21*

Employee Full Name: *Sleeps Her Way to the Top*

Position: *Promotional Director*

Supervisor: *VP of BS*

Payroll: *Superior has flagged her for a substantial increase*

Performance Appraisals: *High marks across the board.*

Regarded as a hard worker who's VERY eager to please. Past

employers have praised her for her excellent ability to anticipate

their urgent needs. However, several infractions reported by fellow

employees for dress code violations.

Training and Development: *Recommended for immediate promotion.*

No training needed.

Employee Relations: *Extremely popular with executive level, but has*

had several unfortunate encounters in the ladies' room with

members of the typing pool.

Can You Hear Me Now?

RISK LEVEL

TARGET: Caffeine Freak

Office Supplies

Phone, shoe polish

This prank is especially sweet to spring on anyone who's expected in a big meeting later or heading out on a sales call. The most important piece of this prank, though, is making sure that the shoe polish you choose matches the phones your company has. Black phones mean black shoe polish, red polish for red phones. You get my drift.

When **Caffeine Freak** saunters off for another cup of coffee, slip into his cube and rub shoe polish liberally on the earpiece of his phone. If you're getting antsy waiting for the fun to happen,

you can always be the one to give him a call later. Just make sure you keep him on the phone for a few minutes, so that the shoe polish really works its way onto his ear.

Fast-track

No polish? No problem. Superglue the phone to the receiver, time it to dry in time for an important conference call.

Wake-Up Call

**RISK
LEVEL**

TARGET: Naps at His Desk

Office Supplies

Intercom

I never had the pleasure of working in an office with a company intercom system, but my cousin Wilber Fired has, so he told me all about this special prank.

Most intercom systems run through the phones and have a special code to get in, usually a simple number like 25 or 99. Before initiating this prank you'll obviously need the code. Then have the **Hot Temp** call **Naps at His Desk** to let him know there's a call on line 99 (or whatever number you need to hit to reach the intercom system). And then hang up. When **Naps at His Desk** sleepily picks up the call and announces his name, his yawns will be broadcast for all to hear.

Toe Jam

TARGET: Hot Temp

RISK LEVEL

Office Supplies
<u>Gum</u>

The **Hot Temp** often keeps extra pairs of shoes at her desk. She may wear sneakers to work and change into her favorite Jimmy Choos when she punches in. Or perhaps she keeps an extra pair in the office, just in case she gets caught in the rain on her commute in.

Spend the day at your desk chewing gum and saving the gobs in their wrappers. Once you've had an opportunity to chew the whole pack, use her time away from her desk to deposit the wads in whatever extra pairs of shoes you can find. Make sure the gooey mess isn't noticeable from a casual inspection. The next time the **Hot Temp** opts for a quick change, she'll be in for a sticky surprise!

Prank Pitfall

The gum can get pretty messy for you, so opt for gummy worms for a similar sticky effect.

Bummer, Dude!

RISK LEVEL

TARGETS: The entire office

Office supplies

A tube of topical heat rub (such as Ben-Gay or Icy Hot)

Get into work early, or wait until most of the office is in an important meeting. Then grab a friend to keep watch and sneak into the restrooms. Using a paper towel or toilet paper, apply the heat rub cream to all the toilet seats. Don't be stingy! Make sure they're generously slathered, but not so much that it's noticeable on the lid.

   Spend the rest of the day watching the whole company rub their backsides and fidget in their seats!

The Write Stuff

TARGET: Stick Up Her Butt

RISK LEVEL

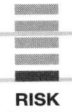

Office supplies

Clear nail polish

When nobody's looking, "borrow" **Stick Up Her Butt's** pen and pencil cup from her desk. Using the clear nail polish, paint the tips of her entire collection. Once you're sure they're dry, return the writing utensils to her desk. Next time she tries to jot something down, she'll think she's writing with invisible ink!

Fast-track

Conversely, loosen all of her pens so that the ink will get everywhere next time she goes to write something.

Clear Coat

Keyboard Caper

RISK LEVEL

TARGET: Old Timer

Office supplies

Letter opener

While **Old Timer** is out at a meeting, help yourself to his computer. You can have a friend keep watch while you go to work. Pop off a number of letters from his keyboard. The letter opener will help give you the leverage you need. Once you're able to get your finger underneath the key, you'll find it comes off quite easily. Once you have enough buttons removed, rearrange them in any order you choose. You can spell out all sorts of messages with them, such as "Gotcha!"

When **Old Timer** returns, his message will be wait-ing for him. Or if he's especially close to re-tirement, he may peck his way through quite a few typos before he notices that something's amiss.

Mission Disorganization

RISK LEVEL

TARGET: Mr. Competitive

Office Supplies

None

While **Mr. Competitive** is out buying the hottest new labelmaker, sneak on over to his desk. Remove all the drawers, switch them up and return them to different locations.

When he gets back from his shopping excursion, **Mr. Competitive** will go batty trying to find his change sorter!

He Who Smelt It...

RISK LEVEL

TARGET: The entire office

Office Supplies

Paper, marker, tape

Write "WHO FARTED?" in big block letters on a sheet of paper. Surreptitiously place the sign and the "roll" of tape in a file folder, then carry it with you to the elevator bank. Hopefully, you'll catch the elevator empty on the first try, but you might need to take a few rides before you get a moment alone. When there are no witnesses, tape the sign securely to the inside of the elevator doors. Make a quick exit.

The next group going up is sure to get a good laugh—while they eye one another suspiciously . . .

Fast-track

Leave a small stink-bomb. Think: Rotten eggs, sauerkraut that's past its prime, gym socks that were in your bag for a week. Get creative!

Suggestive Reading

RISK LEVEL

TARGET: Idiot with All the Power and Sleeps Her Way to the Top

Office Supplies

Your favorite porn magazine (we know—you only read the articles), interoffice envelope

Using an interoffice envelope, mark **Idiot with All the Power** as being the last to receive it. Then address the envelope to **Sleeps Her Way to the Top** and slide your prized bathroom literature inside. Drop it off at a mail station that can't easily be traced back to you.

Who knows? You could instigate the start of a beautiful relationship!

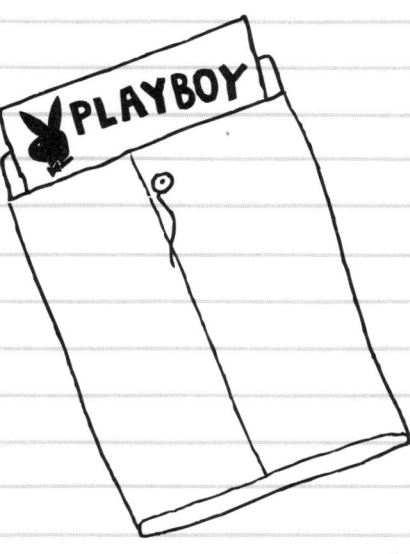

Dead Ringer

RISK LEVEL

TARGET: Talks Too Much and Idiot with All the Power

Office Supplies

Phone

We've all been there. You're trying to get a project finished like a good little worker bee, but you can't concentrate due to all the incessant yapping down the hall. **Talks Too Much** spends eight hours a day talking shoe sales and soap operas with her friends, and nobody seems to notice all the personal calls she's making but you! You need to put a stop to this!

When **Talks Too Much** is out to lunch, forward all of her calls to **Idiot with All the Power's** number. His phone will start ringing off the hook. It won't take long for him to get the picture, and he's sure to pull the plug on **Talks Too Much's** line!

CYA

Blame the crossed wires on the phone repairman.

Printer Error (in Your Favor!)

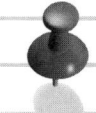

RISK LEVEL

TARGET: The Hypochondriac

Office Supplies

Computer

Chances are your office is linked with a whole network of printers. When **The Hypochondriac** steps away for one of his frequent trips to the restroom, sneak on over to his computer. Go to the "Settings" or "System Preferences" menu and enter "Printer Setup." Quickly choose a new default printer that's as far away from his workstation as possible.

When he comes back, he'll be confounded as to why his WebMD articles to diagnose Alzheimer's just aren't printing. If you get really lucky, **He Who Knows Everything** will happen upon the proof of your target's abuse of computer privileges and report him!

Fast-track

Adjust the settings so his documents print out on letterhead.

Condiment Caper

RISK LEVEL

TARGET: Super Slob

Office Supplies

Ketchup packet

When **Super Slob** carries his latest order from the local grease pit into his office, call him on the intercom to let him know there's a visitor waiting for him on another floor. As he goes to check it out, make your way over to his lunch, ketchup in hand. Tear the corner off of the packet and stick the end of his straw through the opening. Open the drink's lid and insert the ketchup packet (with the straw still attached) into the drink. Then replace the lid with the straw once again poking out the top. Make a hasty exit—but go ahead and help yourself to a French fry first.

When **Super Slob** finally comes back from his wild-goose chase, he'll get a big surprise when he goes to wet his whistle!

Fast-track

Purloin the condiment packs so your target goes for the communal bottle of ketchup. Add about 1 tablespoon of baking soda to the ketchup bottle to make it explode. Stay clear!

Sew Screwed

RISK LEVEL

VICTIM: Hot Temp

Office Supplies

Needle and thread

Save up this prank for the chillier days when the **Hot Temp** shows up in her expensive new outerwear. While she's off powdering her nose, swipe the jacket and get to work. You don't have to be Martha Stewart for this sewing project. All you have to do is bring both sleeves forward to the coat's front and pass the needle and thread through the ends of both the sleeves. Once you've made enough stitches to hold the sleeves firmly together, put the jacket back where you found it.

The **Hot Temp** will have the darnedest time slipping her jacket on that evening. Not to worry, though, the stitches will easily be snipped out without causing any permanent damage. So tell her to chill out!

CYA

Blame it on the Crafty Spinster in the office.

Revolving Doors

RISK LEVEL

TARGET: The entire office

Office Supplies

Paper, marker, tape

Get up bright and early one morning and start working on your signs. Calculate the number of exterior doors to your office building and make enough "Please Use Other Door" signs for each entrance. (Don't forget to make two signs for double doors.)

Be sure to get to work before anyone else and tape the signs securely to all the doors. Now you can take your bagel and coffee upstairs to your office and have a leisurely breakfast while you wait to see how long it takes your coworkers to find their way inside.

Sweat Equity

For maximum pranking effect, stay late and print on letterhead the night before; arrive early and post in the A.M.

When the Cat's Away ...

**RISK
LEVEL**

TARGET: Clueless

Office Supplies

Computer

When **Clueless** goes for a
smoke, mosey on over to
his computer. Click on
the "Settings" or "System
Preferences" menu and then
go to "Mouse Controls."
Set the mouse tracking
speed to the slowest pos-
sible position, then close
up the windows and go back
to your desk.

Clueless won't have any
idea what's wrong with
his computer. Inevitably,
the IT guy will have to
be called down to fix the
little snafu.

CYA

Blame the new Operating
System, or Corporate
IT for reconfiguring all
the settings from afar.

WIDGET/TEX PERSONNEL FILE
PERSONAL AND CONFIDENTIAL

Date: *April 1*

Employee Full Name: *Kisses the Boss's Ass*

Position: *Assistant Manager*

Supervisor: *Big Boss Man*

Payroll: *Up for an increase Q1 next year*

Performance Appraisals: *Q1 performance appraisal came in with a glowing report. Employee is punctual, helpful, organized, and fluent in three languages. Also reported as being "quirky" and "strangely unpopular" with support staff.*

Training and Development: *Employee recommended for training to move to next level.*

Employee Relations: *Very popular with executive level but recently cited for disrupting a meeting with a tray of donuts.*

Get a Life

RISK LEVEL

TARGET: Kisses the Boss's Ass

Office Supplies

Pen, calendar

Kisses the Boss's Ass is always talking about how much work he has, how many meetings he attends, and how little time he has to get it all done. It's time to teach **Kisses the Boss's Ass** that things could be much worse.

When he steps out of his office, sneak on over to his business calendar and add a few things to his "to do" list. Next Monday schedule a "Widget Assessment Meeting," make Thursday the boss's birthday, and throw in an appointment with his proctologist on Friday. Fill up **Kisses the Boss's Ass's** calendar as much as possible. It's a good thing he doesn't have a life! There's no time for one!

Time Change

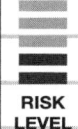

RISK LEVEL

TARGET: Clock Watcher

Office Supplies
Computer

Every office has a **Clock Watcher**. He's the guy that comes in at 9:00 A.M. on the button and doesn't stay a second past 5:00 P.M. It doesn't matter if the rest of the department is staying late to finish a project, he puts in just enough time to keep his job. Well, until now . . .

Keep an eye out and take notice when **Clock Watcher** isn't wearing his watch one day (they all need new batteries at some point, right?). That's the only day this prank will truly work, so be alert! When he steps away for one of his ten-minute (not a second less) smoke breaks, mosey on over to his computer. Go to "Clock" on the "System Preferences" or "Settings" menu and set time backward about forty-five minutes. If he has anything else that tells time in his office, be sure to futz with those as well! Slink back to your cubicle.

Thanks to you, **Clock Watcher** sits at his desk long after everyone else has left!

Searching for Trouble

RISK LEVEL

TARGET: Hot Temp

Office Supplies

Computer

The **Hot Temp** spends almost all of her workday online. She shops for purses, posts on message boards, and catches up on all of her friends' blogs. Google is **Hot Temp's** best friend. Wouldn't it be a shame if they had a communication breakdown?

When **Hot Temp** heads out to mail her latest online auction sale at lunchtime, slip on over to her desk. Open her web browser (chances are there's already several windows open) and go to Google. Click on "Preferences," then go to the drop-down menu next to "Interface Language". Choose "Hacker," then click on "Save Preferences." Quickly close the window.

The next time **Hot Temp** conducts a search, she'll be greeted with a bunch of gibberish. This can be a tough glitch to fix, because now all the language preferences will be illegible and it will take her a number of attempts to find her way back to English.

Party Line

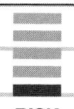

RISK LEVEL

TARGETS: Nervous Nelly and Super Slob

Office Supplies

Phone

This is a prank you can pull on two victims at once! Double the fun!

   Call **Nervous Nelly** on your office phone. When she picks up, immediately conference in **Super Slob**. Then be very, very quiet. A little giggle or even some heavy breathing will give the whole thing away. Each of them will think the other person called them. They're likely to get irritated pretty quickly, or maybe . . . just maybe . . .
you've created a love con-
nection!

One Hot Ride

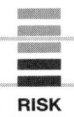

RISK LEVEL

TARGET: Mr. Competitive

Office Supplies

Paper, pen

Mr. Competitive finally saved up enough money to trade in his Subaru for a Mustang convertible. And he's very proud of it. So proud he goes out and polishes his "baby" every lunch hour with a cloth diaper.

Before the end of the workday, duck out of the office building for a few minutes and place a note on **Mr. Competitive's** windshield. It should read something like this:

"I'm so sorry for the ding. I had trouble seeing your car out the back of my SUV and only realized I hit when I heard the crunch. Rest assured my insurance company will pay for everything!"

Leave the note unsigned. That evening you're sure to witness **Mr. Competitive** scrambling around his car, sweating profusely and desperately looking for the point of the collision.

The Crying Game

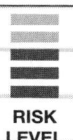

TARGET: The entire office

RISK LEVEL

Office Supplies

Plastic sandwich bag, hot peppers, tissues

Here's your chance to afflict the whole office with a case of the weepies.

Bring a sandwich bag full of hot peppers into work one day. Crush them up as best you can then apply the juice and pulp to all the public door handles. Be sure to wash your hands after you've finished.

Throughout the course of the day, as the juice gets rubbed into sleepy eyes, the whole office will suffer a crying jag. Be sure to have large boxes of tissues in your office and offer sympathy.

Attack of the Killer Tomatoes

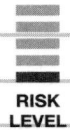

RISK LEVEL

TARGET: Whoever comes along at just the right time

Office Supplies

Ketchup packets, tape

This is a great booby trap that can surprise whichever unsuspecting coworker happens along first!

To heat: Tape a bunch of ketchup packets to the top inside part of the microwave, where they'll likely go unnoticed. The next person to heat something up will witness a bloodbath like no other as the ketchup packets explode all over the inside . . . and your victim's lunch!

CYA

Blame Super Slob by saying he's trying to get back at you for the other ketchup prank— touché!

A Pack a Day Keeps the Pranks Away

TARGET: Old Timer

RISK LEVEL

Office Supplies

A tube of numbing gel (such as Orajel)

You're sick to death of being able to smell smokey **Old Timer** all the way down the hall. Of course, he doesn't light up in the office anymore, but his clothes, skin, hair, and office reek of butts. Maybe it's time to give him even more incentive to kick the habit!

When **Old Timer** has ducked out of his office and left his pack of cigarettes behind, sneak in, armed with your tube of numbing gel. Quickly empty the pack and rub a thin coat of the gel on the cigarette's end that will rest on **Old Timer's** lips.

Neatly return the smokes to their wrapper and get on out of there.

As **Old Timer** makes his way through the pack, his lips will become more and more tingly. He may start to worry that it's a side effect and consult his doctor! With any luck, you just helped him kick the habit!

Find a Penny, Pick It Up— If You Can

RISK LEVEL

TARGET: The next coworker to come along

Office Supplies

A quarter, super glue

This quintessential prank never gets old. It should, but it doesn't. What makes this prank extra special is that instead of targeting just one victim you're bound to get hours of pleasure through multiple victims.

All you need to do to get this prank rolling is super glue a quarter to the floor. Unfortunately, inflation has made a penny no longer good enough. I think that for a couple of hours of fun you can splurge and use a quarter. After all, who's going to make the effort to stop for a penny? The trick is choosing your floor space. If you're blessed enough to have a company cafeteria or lunchroom, this is perfect. If not, I suggest space around a vending machine. Few things make quarters more valuable than vending machines. Unless, maybe, parking meters.

The real beauty of this prank is it could go on for days, until someone finally gets on their hands and knees and pries that sucker off.

I Heart Spam

RISK LEVEL

TARGET: Idiot with All the Power

Office supplies

E-mail address

There are few things more annoying than an e-mail inbox full of newsletters, but what better prank than an e-mail inbox full of newsletters? The great thing about this is that you don't even need to leave your own desk. Perfect for the lazy prankster!

All you need to do is sign up **Idiot with All the Power** to every e-mail newsletter you come across, and of course I suggest you seek out a few good ones on your own. Maybe he'd like to hear more about tips for the new bride, sex vacations, nude beaches, imported cars, ferret care, child care, or foot health. Whatever you come across in your random search, sign him up. He'll be thrilled to learn more about the capybara—the world's largest rodent.

Band of Rubbers

RISK LEVEL

TARGET: Stick Up Her Butt

Office Supplies

Scissors

Stick Up Her Butt is so perfect she even insists on color-coded rubberbands. Only use the red ones for financial reports and the white ones for sales figures. Annoying! Like you have nothing better to do than remember which color rubberband goes with which report. After one of those long drawn-out days where **Stick Up Her Butt** chastises you again for using the wrong rubberband it's time for a little sweet revenge.

While she's away planning the next office party, you can slip into her rubberband desk drawer, the one with little color-coded boxes for the different rubberband colors, and using a scissors snip away. Snip, snip, snip. It won't be long before there isn't a fully intact rubberband in the drawer. And then sit back and watch her frustration as she struggles to find the perfect red rubberband.

We Must Have Crossed Lines

RISK LEVEL

TARGET: Conspiracy Theorist and Mr. Competitive

Office Supplies

None

This is one of the few pranks that allows you to get two people at once. Unfortunately it's only going to work with the right office configuration. To successfully pull this off you need to have an open office where desks are set up back-to-back and employees face each other. I've personally never worked in an office like this and can't imagine looking at anyone's ugly mug all day every day.

This is a fun one to pull on **Conspiracy Theorist** and **Mr. Competitive**. While both are away simply slip in and switch their monitor cables. That way when they sit down at their desks **Conspiracy Theorist** will see what should be on **Mr. Competitive's** monitor. Watch the confusion, the panic, and the call to IT as **Conspiracy Theorist** is convinced that somehow **Mr. Competitive** has been hacking into his private records.

A Little Personal Space, Please

RISK LEVEL

TARGETS: Idiot with All the Power and his entire staff

Office supplies

Company letterhead

A great prank for the entire office. It's guaranteed to rile things up, and there's no question that by the time **Idiot with All the Power** is able to take control the day has already been shot.

Personal calls and e-mails are a right to every office worker looking to kill a little time. How else are you supposed to plan Friday night or find out what he was really thinking when he said that? And while all offices have "strict" rules against personal calls and e-mail we all know that no one ever enforces it, unless of course you're calling your girlfriend in Taiwan.

This time though, things are about to change. Your office memo is announcing a new office policy that no longer allows personal calls or e-mails. Phones and computers will be strictly monitored by the newly hired Personal Guard and anyone breaking the rule is subject to immediate dismissal. The company however is not completely immune to the fact that employees do, at times, need to make personal contacts. Therefore, instead of using the phone or e-mail, a schedule has been established for personal visits only, times when each employee is allowed one guest to handle any personal problems. Include the schedule in your memo, giving each employee a fifteen-minute personal slot. And then sit back and watch the hysteria ensue. It won't be long before a line forms outside the boss's door with complaints that an 8 A.M. time slot will never work or that fifteen minutes isn't enough time. There's nothing better than a whiff of big brother to send everyone into a panic.

Pranks Unplugged

RISK LEVEL

TARGET: Forever an Assistant

Office Supplies

Keyboard or mouse

This is always a fun prank and especially good for **Forever an Assistant**, the employee who thinks he's much more important than he really is. All you need to do is slip into his desk one day while he's away and unplug his mouse, his keyboard, or both and watch the panic. It's amazing how long it takes for people to look into the obvious (whether or not things are plugged in) and instead spend a great deal of time shutting down, turning on, calling IT, and just plain panicking.

The Art of Dribbling

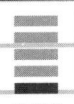

RISK LEVEL

TARGET: The next person in line

Office Supplies

Paper cups, a sharp pin

One day, while you're sitting around with nothing better to do, head to the office kitchen and grab a stack of paper coffee cups. Instead of surfing the web to waste time, spend valuable hours poking a small hole in the top of each cup, near the lip—not big enough to be noticed, but definitely big enough to make a mess.

Of course not everyone is going to get dribbled on, since it will depend which way the hole faces when you drink, but enough will to make this prank fun. And the really fun part is that no one will ever know when the prank ends or if the cup they have is a dribbler.

You might just want to make sure that you pick your own cup early on and don't let it get out of sight or thrown away!

Sweat Equity

This is a prank that could go on for months if you really want to put in the work.

Touch and Die

RISK LEVEL

TARGET: Stick Up Her Butt

Office Supplies

Access to your victim's favorite items

In every office there's one **Stick Up Her Butt**, the coworker who insists that no one touch her dictionary, pen, or notebook. Even when asked, she won't loan out a pen, a company-paid-for pen, because she's afraid someone might run off with it. She's the one who makes sure her name is on every last one of her office supplies (even those found in her office when she first started six years ago).

Well it's easy to wreak havoc in the world of good ol' **Stick Up Her Butt**. All you need to do is take her favorite dictionary, her prized pen, or even that weird action figurine she keeps on her desk for a spin about town. When you do, don't forget your camera. Photos of her figurine riding the shopping mall escalator and eating at Sbaro will give her heart palpitations. Let the game go on for a week, a month, or as long as the joke lasts. The truly ambitious can set up a website so that everyone can watch the figurine antics. Others might be happy with random photos sent via e-mail or left on her desk.

Lunch Is on You

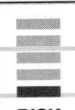

RISK LEVEL

TARGET: Mooch

Office Supplies

Phone

The perfect prank for **Mooch**, the guy who never seems to have his wallet on him and the first to appear when free snacks are laid out. Make a quick call to the local pizza parlor and place a lunchtime order for one large anchovy pizza. Or, better yet, place an order to satisfy the entire office—a large stack of deliciously fishy pizzas—all under the name **Mooch**. When the delivery guy comes and asks for **Office Mooch**, he'll have no choice but to pay the guy! Maybe this time everyone else will get a free treat.

Duration

Do this once a week with a different pizza joint each time. Start out with one pizza, and by the fourth week, have 6 or more pies delivered and watch Mooch weep!

Happy UnBirthday to You

RISK LEVEL

TARGET: Idiot with All the Power

Office Supplies

None

Office lunches always sound like fun, until you're actually sitting around the table at the local franchise pub and it dawns on you that this is just another meeting—chips and salsa don't make any difference. Just because you're out of your office environment doesn't mean you aren't capable of pulling off a great stunt! Remember, these people are counting on you to liven things up. Excuse yourself to go to the loo and corner your waiter to let him know that today is **Idiot with All the Power's** birthday and you want all the bells and whistles—singing, clapping, an exploding cake. Bring it on!

Fast-track

Spread it around the office ahead of time that it's Idiot's birthday, and have everyone sign a card and chip in for a gift. (More money for the pranking pool!)

Subscribe Me

RISK LEVEL

TARGET: A little something for everyone

Office Supplies

Pen

The next time you're at Walgreens, take a spin through the magazine section and grab as many of those little magazine subscription cards as possible. Pick up *Cat Fancy* for **Mr. Competitive**, *Martha Stewart Living* for **Super Slob**, and *Guns and Ammo* for **Nervous Nelly**. Just remember, the fun only happens if the new magazines are actually sent to them at the office.

Fast-track

If you're feeling a little crazy, start a subscription to Penthouse in Idiot with All the Power's name (sent to the office, of course)!

Spice Things Up!

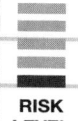

RISK LEVEL

TARGET: Mooch

Office Supplies

Office kitchen bottle of ketchup

The office refrigerator is a great source of pranks and one that should never be overlooked. Have you ever considered all the fun you can have with a bottle of hot sauce? Well I have, and here's just one possibility for you to consider. If you're one of those offices actively promoting greener living, it's very likely you have a community ketchup bottle, in an attempt to try and eliminate all of those little packets that will end up lying around. If so, you're in luck with this prank. One day, when you find yourself alone in the kitchen, whip out your handy bottle of Tabasco and add a dash or 200 to the ketchup. Give it a quick shake and order a bag of fries for everyone to share. If you're not lucky enough to have community ketchup, buy a bottle, spice it up, and stick it in the fridge. There's no doubt that **Mooch** will be there to take a swig in less time than it takes for you to say, "hands off."

A Curdle in the Morning

RISK LEVEL

TARGET: Caffeine Freak, et al.

Office Supplies

Bottle of lemon juice

The great thing about this prank is that it's one that can go on for weeks or even months, so head to Costco to get your lemon juice because you might be needing it for a very long time. Your biggest target with this is going to be **Caffeine Freak**, but really it's a prank that will get anyone who drinks milk with her coffee or tea, or eats a bowl of cereal at her desk in the morning.

At the end of the day, slip into the kitchen and add a generous squirt of lemon juice to each carton of milk or cream you find in the fridge. By let-ting them sit overnight you're guaranteed that they will all be nicely curdled in the morning. Then wait a day or two and begin again. Soon you'll have calls in to Human Resources for a new fridge and arguments over who is drinking my milk and leaving me with their old, expired curdled crap. Brilliant!

All Systems Not Go

RISK LEVEL

TARGET: The entire office

Office Supplies

Access to the office's power cords

An easy prank, but one with excellent consequences. While simple and definitely doable for the novice prankster, this is one that's going to take a little bit of time and thought. In fact, you'll probably need to slip into the office one night when everyone has left for the day. When you do, simply go around from desk to desk and unplug everything. We're talking every phone, computers, radios, clocks, **Hypochondriac's** humidifier, **Conspiracy Theorist's** police scanner, and more.

The best part of this prank is that you won't be expected to work for hours the next day, when they can finally get things back up and running, and you'll get to watch the panic and confusion as everyone from IT to maintenance tries to figure out what has gone wrong.

Prank Pitfall

Identify any hidden security cameras in your office and try to avoid being caught on tape; otherwise your path to a pink slip will be hastened.

Firing the First Shot

RISK LEVEL

TARGET: Nervous Nelly

Office Supplies

Computer

Nervous Nelly is almost too easy a target—the slightest problem sends her over the edge—but c'mon, is it really fair to leave her out of the fun? That's why this is the perfect prank to pull on her. While she's away fretting over another office meeting, slip into her seat and take a quick screen shot. The method of doing this will differ from office to office depending on the computer system you're using; therefore, as with all computer pranks, I recommend you test it out on your own computer before sitting down at someone else's desk. Once you have the screen shot done, move all of her desktop items into a folder on her hard drive, call it something clever like, "Gotcha" or "Hey, idiot, we're over here."

When all of that is done, make the screen shot her desktop wallpaper picture. I promise you that it will take hours for **Nervous Nelly**, and even the IT guys, to figure out exactly what happened and why nothing is working.

WIDGET/TEX PERSONNEL FILE
PERSONAL AND CONFIDENTIAL

Date: *September 15*

Employee Full Name: *Nervous Nelly*

Position: *Administrative Assistant, Accounting*

Supervisor: *Conspiracy Theorist*

Payroll: *Cost of living increase approved*

Performance Appraisals: *Superior noted that appraisal had to be performed over three meetings as employee requested to be excused to the restroom the first time and never returned. At second meeting, employee was sweating profusely and had to leave the room after depleting her supervisor's tissue supply.*

Training and Development: *Employee is a hard worker, but contributes little to planning meetings. Not expected to advance beyond this position.*

Employee Relations: *Mostly keeps to herself. But does not garner coworker complaints.*

Where's the Buzz?

RISK LEVEL

TARGET: Caffeine Freak

Office Supplies
Decaf coffee, followed by espresso!

This prank will have you snickering at your desk for weeks. It's great fun for the entire office! Watch **Caffeine Freak** freak out when he can't keep his head up for meetings.

Sneak into the break room and replace the caffeinated coffee supplies with decaf. Then put on a pot and watch the snooze-fest begin! Make sure you have a good supply of asprin on hand for when those caffeine headaches set in.

Then, when everyone just starts adjusting, switch to espresso and get out of the way!

Starving in America

RISK LEVEL

TARGET: Everyone needing a sugar fix

Office Supplies

Vending machine

You'll want to wait until mid- to late afternoon for this easy prank. Sneak over to the vending machine and unplug it. See how long it takes for the afternoon slump to drive people crazy with sugar cravings.

Fast-track

To make everyone a little crazier, stock up on sugary goodies. When your coworkers ask, tell them you got 'em from the vending machine (when you really got them on the way to work)!

Secret Meetings

RISK LEVEL

TARGET: He Who Knows Everything

Office Supplies

Letterhead

Here's a simple prank to relieve your tension on a boring day in Office Land.

Use company letterhead to write a memo calling a meeting for a time when everyone who's anyone is out of the office. Leave the memo on **He Who Knows Everything's** desk and watch him panic when he thinks he's got the wrong location. Watch him run around frantically, trying to find out where he went wrong.

Variation

This prank also works well if there is an actual meeting scheduled and you change the meeting location on He Who Knows Everything's copy of the memo.

It's a Holly, Jolly Christmas

RISK LEVEL

TARGET: Mr. Competitive, He Who Knows Everything, or Naps at His Desk

Office Supplies

Letterhead

It's not the holiday season without a few festive pranks thrown in. How about rescheduling the company Christmas party . . . for just a select few coworkers (your favorites!). Create a memo from the **Big Boss Man** moving the party to a swanky restaurant where you know a private party is being held at the same time. Think how **Mr. Competitive**, **He Who Knows Everything**, or **Naps at His Desk** will feel when they show up in their Christmas colors at the wrong place, at the wrong time. Ho, ho, ho!

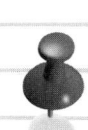

Good Grief

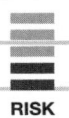

RISK LEVEL

TARGET: Kisses the Boss's Ass

Office Supplies

None

This prank will not win you any popularity contests. It's a mean trick, but it will certainly put **Kisses the Boss's Ass** in a very awkward position.

When the boss goes on vacation, inform your gullible coworker that he's out for a death in the family. Show her the sympathy card you're sending to the boss's home address. **Kisses the Boss's Ass** is sure to make a Hallmark run and end up digging her own grave!

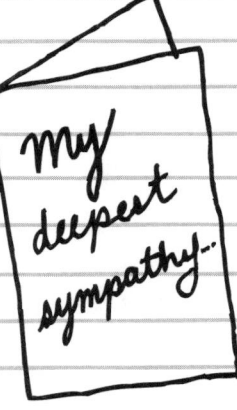

my deepest sympathy...

Say Cheese!

RISK LEVEL

TARGET: Woeful Wallflower

Office Supplies

Photos of yourself

Since you are so much better looking than the others in the office, you might want to share the wealth. Steal into **Woeful Wallflower's** cubicle and tape your photos over her family photos. Of course, you might end up with a new "friend," but other pranks can nip that relationship in the bud pronto!

CYA

Instead of pics of yourself, tape up the mug of the latest in-the-news political figure and blame the **Conspiracy Theorist**.

Keyboard Unplugged

RISK LEVEL

TARGET: Clueless

Office Supplies

None

This one is almost too easy! Wait until **Clueless** is out on a coffee break and sneak into his office. Use your crafty accomplice as a lookout. Unplug the keyboard from the computer. He'll have IT in his office before you know it. For an extra fun trick, hide his keyboard altogether and see how long it takes him to even notice it's missing!

CYA

Come up with a wild tale and see if Clueless falls for it: Blame office "ghosts" for unplugging and hiding your keyboard.

Counting Every Minute

RISK LEVEL

TARGET: Mr. Competitive

Office Supplies

None

Wait until you and **Mr. Competitive** are in a long meeting: You know the kind; it goes on and on and on. Tell **Mr. Competitive** that the **Big Boss Man** asked him to take detailed minutes of the meeting and present them to him by the end of the day. Office sabotage: Gotta love it!

Fast-track

Tell Mr. Competitive that he'll need to present his notes to whatever group isn't present at the meeting the following day. Get an accomplice to corroborate your story …

Will the Real Boss Please Stand Up?

RISK LEVEL

TARGET: Forever an Assistant or Naps at His Desk

Office supplies

Office memo paper

Send out a memo from the boss stating that it's Dress Like the Boss Day. Leave it on your coworkers' desks at the end of the day on a Friday so they have the weekend to prepare. This trick is best if you target a few gullible employees like **Forever an Assistant** or **Naps at His Desk**. When Monday comes, watch the fireworks!

— Behind Every Good Man — Is His Boss's Family

RISK LEVEL

TARGET: Conspiracy Theorist or Sleeps Her Way to the Top

Office Supplies

None

Some days you're just not up for a lot of effort, but you do have a reputation to uphold. On those lazy prankster days, perpetrate this photo op on an unsuspecting coworker.

Sneak into **Conspiracy Theorist's** cubicle and switch his family photos with the boss's family photos. See who notices first! **Sleeps Her Way to the Top** is also a good choice for this one. There's nothing like a few uncomfortable moments to get a slow Monday off to a good start.

Switch Hitter

RISK LEVEL

TARGET: Stick Up Her Butt and Super Slob

Office Supplies

Letterhead

Create an office memo telling a few select co-workers that the next day is Switch Department Day. In an effort to foster interoffice harmony, you will be switching departments and desks so you can walk in your coworker's shoes. Send it to a few workers who you know will get to work early enough to beat out the people whose desks they will be working at. Involving **Stick Up Her Butt** and the **Super Slob** and other polar opposites makes this a hoot and half.

Hello, My Name Is—

RISK LEVEL

TARGET: Kisses the Boss's Ass

Office Supplies

Letterhead

New office policy! Starts tomorrow! Everyone must wear a nametag to foster office camaraderie. After work, leave the memo on a few selected coworkers' desks, along with the nametags. **Kisses the Boss's Ass** is sure to comply.

Nothing Is Too Personal

RISK LEVEL

TARGET: Nervous Nelly

Office Supplies

Letterhead

This trick is for the truly brave, laugh-in-the-face-of-fear prankster. Craft a memo to **Nervous Nelly** that says the boss has asked that she open all the boss's mail from now on. Effective immediately. Then get out of the way (and get a lawyer), fast!

File, File, Toil, and Trouble

RISK LEVEL

TARGET: Forever an Assistant

Office Supplies

Letterhead

Who doesn't love a chance to help out the boss? Really, you'll be doing your coworker a favor by setting up this trick. Leave a note on **Forever an Assistant's** desk from the boss telling her she wants her files all reorganized. Timing is the key to this prank. Set it up to start during lunch when the boss is out of the office.

When the boss gets back to the office, she's greeted with a File Disaster Area. Run!

Tide-al Wave

RISK LEVEL

TARGET: Kisses the Boss's Ass

Office Supplies

Letterhead

Kisses the Boss's Ass just loves to be helpful. He loves to get ahead, using any and all opportunities that come his way. He won't be able to resist this one!

Leave a memo from the boss on **Kisses the Boss's Ass's** desk asking him to take home the boss's dirty gym clothes at the end of the day to wash them. What's more fun than having your coworker wash your boss's dirty gym socks? Not much, believe me. But the boss may not be quite as grateful as your unsuspecting target might expect.

Bun in the Oven

TARGET: He Who Knows Everything

RISK LEVEL

Office Supplies

None

Ahhh, the perfect prank for **He Who Knows Everything,** who has driven you mad these last few years. Tell the smarty pants that your female boss just announced her pregnancy. Watch as the boss's face turns red with indignation as he insults her with his congratulations.

CYA

Blame that Chatty Kathy over in Publicity, Talks Too Much.

A Special Holiday Just for You

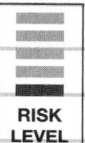

RISK LEVEL

TARGET: Kisses the Boss's Ass

Office Supplies

Letterhead

This is a great way to set **Kisses the Boss's Ass** back a rung or two on the ladder to success. Send a memo from the boss announcing alternating holidays, but make sure you only include those holidays that you don't traditionally have off. For instance, the boss might announce that she wants everyone in the department to take different holidays off. X, Y, and Z can take Martin Luther King Day (even though the office is really open), while A, B, and C take Presidents' Day (because no one honors the presidents anymore).

Send the memo just before the upcoming holiday that you want **Kisses the Boss's Ass** to take advantage of. See how long it takes the boss to call her when she doesn't show up for works. Oops.

Time for a Shower?

RISK LEVEL

TARGET: The next one through the door

Office Supplies
Rubberband

This is good for a belly laugh to relieve your tension after a long afternoon in the Bored Room. It's the perfect prank for the next sucker to come along—doesn't matter who it is! The genius of the trick is that it's so simple and it's tough to get caught.

Check out the sink in the break room or kitchen to make sure it has a spray attachment. Take a rubberband and put it around the sprayer's lever so that the sprayer will be activated whenever someone turns on the water. Make sure to aim the sprayer up into the general vicinity of the victim's face. Stand back and enjoy the shower!

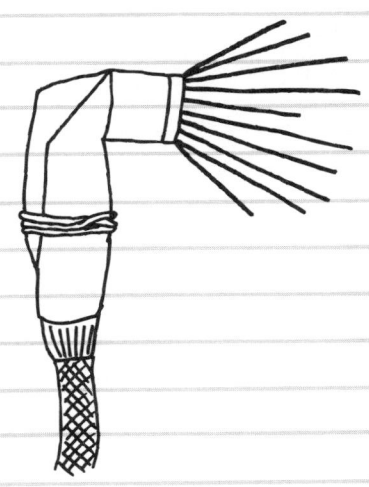

Grease Her Up

RISK LEVEL

TARGET: Stick Up Her Butt

Office Supplies

Vaseline

Stick Up Her Butt likes everything just so. She's squeamish and very particular with just about everything. When she's out of her office running errands run over, close her office door, and coat her doorknob with Vaseline. Ewwww!

Fast-track

Why stop there? Lube up her phone earpiece, handles to her file cabinet, get creative!

Scrolling Pink Slip

RISK LEVEL

TARGET: Stick Up Her Butt or Clueless

Office Supplies

Computer

This is the perfect prank for **Stick Up Her Butt** or **Clueless**. It's especially perfect for all of your fellow drones who sit in a cube out in the open (can you say Torture?). When you know your patsy will be out at a long lunch (especially one with drinks involved, which will nicely impair function) or in afternoon meetings, change his scrolling marquis to say something like: "The Boss Sucks" or "I Love Kitty Kats."

Snack Attack

RISK LEVEL

TARGET: Anyone who is truly annoying you

Office Supplies

Letterhead

I was thinking at first I would choose **Talks Too Much** for this, but then again, really, **Kisses the Boss's Ass** is probably the perfect choice.

Your mission will have to be pulled off on a day when **Kisses the Boss's Ass** is out of the office. So when he's run out to collect **Idiot with All the Power's** dry cleaning or is buttering up a semi-important client, you can hit the ground running. Type up a memo for distribution officewide announcing that on the following Monday, a new vending machine will be installed. Apologize for the short notice, but let everyone know that for the first time the company is asking for input on the types of snacks that will be included. All requests will have to be in by the end of the day and should be called in to **Kisses the Boss's Ass** at whatever his extension might be. Imagine his surprise when he returns to work and has to listen to hundreds of messages that simply say things like, "Snickers" or "Rollos."

Never Too Sweet

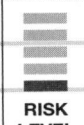

RISK LEVEL

TARGET: Caffeine Freak

Office Supplies

Sugar packets

This prank is perfect for **Caffeine Freak**, your high-strung coworker who never goes anywhere without a fresh brewed cuppa joe in hand. Take advantage of that quiet moment when **Caffeine Freak** wanders away from his coffee and quickly dump a packet or twelve of sugar in the cup. Watch his horror when he comes back and takes that first fortifying sip.

Fast-track

Feeling diabolical? Add pepper instead of sugar!

Who's Lurking at the Door?

TARGET: Talks Too Much

RISK LEVEL

Office Supplies

A pair of dress shoes (even better if they look like the boss's)

Talks Too Much is busy on the phone . . . again. She's loud enough to disturb even the deafest coworker and never knows when to quit. Well, now it's your turn to get her back.

Once she's settled in on a real call, you know, one that actually relates to her job and she can't get off easily, place the shoes outside of her door with the tips just peeking around the corner so she can see them. And then listen to her confusion as she wonders who is hovering outside her door and how she can get off the call faster.

Paranoia Will Destroy Ya

RISK LEVEL

TARGET: Mr. Competitive

Office Supplies

None

Doesn't **Mr. Competitive** just drive you crazy? Every hair in place, his nose in the air, and his air of superiority. It's enough to make the perfect prankster crave a little fun.

And THIS is a fun one—a prank that could go on for weeks, months, or as long as it takes to send **Mr. Competitive** straight into therapy.

Keep a close eye on his habits and every time he leaves his desk sneak over and rearrange everything. Just a little. Not enough so that it's obvious to everyone, but enough that when he reaches for his pencil cup it's not exactly in the same place . . . just a few inches off. The next time, shift his plant and the next time, his paperclip holder.

Before long, **Mr. Competitive** is going to wonder if he's losing his mind!

Excuse Me, I Thought You Were a Man

RISK LEVEL

TARGET: The entire office

Office Supplies

None

This prank really works best if the bathrooms signs in your office building are of the magnetic variety. These strips come off easily so you can switch the signs: Men's Room goes to the Women's Room and vice versa. Step back and watch the chaos!

One Man's Trash . . .

RISK LEVEL

TARGET: You—if you're not careful

Office Supplies

Paper, computer, trash bin, tape

This one's good for a few harmless laughs. Use your computer to create a sign that says "In." Print it out and tape it to the side of your trashcan. Then remove your real in-box and replace it with your trashcan on top of the desk.

TP Emergency

RISK LEVEL

TARGET: Stick Up Her Butt

Office Supplies

None

While everyone is out at lunch one day sneak in and steal all the toilet paper from the bathrooms. You'll be sure to drive **Stick Up Her Butt** absolutely out of her mind. But watch out, **Super Slob** might not notice at all! Make sure you save a little for yourself!

CYA

If anyone asks you, tell them you heard they were cutting back on all office supplies, perhaps TP was on the list?

WIDGET/TEX PERSONNEL FILE
PERSONAL AND CONFIDENTIAL

Date: *April 1*

Employee Full Name: *Mae B. Fired*

Position: *Office Drone in Sales Department*

Supervisor: *Idiot with All the Power*

Hired: *October 4*   Fired: *October 6*   Rehired: *February 5*

Payroll: *Up for an increase Q1 next year*

Performance Appraisals: *Q1 performance appraisal recommended employee for psychological testing. Full battery. Awaiting results. Employee is reportedly mean-spirited, mischievous, disruptive, and diabolical. IQ tests reportedly off the charts. This employee is a genius.*

Training and Development: *No training needed. Employee is suited for position and capable of high performance but is reported as being frequently distracted.*

Employee Relations: *Poor*

WIDGET/TEX PERSONNEL FILE—*SIDE 2*
PERSONAL AND CONFIDENTIAL

Date: *April 1*

Employee Full Name: *Mae B. Fired*

Suggestion status reports: *Employee has been cited for Conduct*

Unbecoming by the following department heads:

* *Human Resources*

* *Mailroom*

* *Sales*

* *Cafeteria Staff*

Despite numerous complaints, Miss Fired is also extremely

popular with nonmanagement and is known to boost morale for

support staff. Recommend keeping a close watch.

Note to self: *Follow up with counsel on status of lawsuit*

Rude Awakening

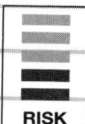

RISK LEVEL

TARGET: Caffeine Freak

Office Supplies

Office sugar bowl

Every busy prankster needs
quick and dirty tricks
that can be played in a
pinch. This will be par-
ticularly effective for
Caffeine Freak, but you'll
be able to get all those
caffeine fans in one shot.
Simply replace all the
sugar in the break room
sugar bowl with salt. Be
sure to turn on the sweet-
ness when your coworkers
revolt!

I've Got Your Number

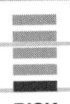

RISK LEVEL

TARGET: Nervous Nelly

Office Supplies

Blank Rolodex cards

Wait until **Nervous Nelly** is out of the office on a coffee break or lunch date. Sneak into her space and "borrow" a few cards from the Rolodex. Create new ones for the ones you take, replicating them except for the phone numbers. The next time she dials the clients' numbers, she'll call the local adult bookstore, the police department, and the funeral home.

Sweat Equity

Make the job easy-breezy by putting the same number on all cards: 867-5309 (maybe Jenny will answer)!

Single White Paper Pusher

RISK LEVEL

TARGET: Stick Up Her Butt, Conspiracy Theorist, or Old Timer

Office supplies

Computer

This is no time to hold back. If you're going for it, go all the way!

Create a profile for **Stick Up Her Butt, Conspiracy Theorist,** or **Old Timer** and post it on some special dating websites with their office e-mail address posted for contact. The crazier the site, the better the results. Who knows, maybe someone in the state pen will find his one and only!

Keep the legal aid number on hand for this one. You could find yourself in a boatload of trouble. And who knows? Maybe *you'll* be the one with newfound friends in the Big House.

Middle Management Mayhem

**Moving up in the world means paying your dues.
Congratulations! You've been promoted.**

Congratulations! You deserve a promotion.
You're no longer the guy getting the
coffee, but now you have some lackey to
do it for you. Let's face it though,
middle management might sound good on
paper, but if you're not careful you
could be stuck there for life . . .
working for the dimwits above you and
training the untrainables below you.
Liven things up with a prank or two and
remember: You're your *own* boss now.

Bring Your Pet to Work Day

RISK LEVEL

TARGET: Animal owners

Office Supplies

Letterhead, copier

This prank is for the truly gullible. The kind of person who looks up gullible in the dictionary when you tell them it's no longer there. Every animal lover in the office will appreciate this one, especially the dog owner with the most ill-behaved dog. You may want to stock up on deodorizer cleaner for the mess that is sure to be left behind!

One night after work, put a "memo" on your co-workers' desks letting people know that Friday will be Bring Your Pet to Work Day and everyone should participate. Make sure to leave the memo off key people's desks, like the **Idiot with All the Power.**

In Case of Emergency, Use Stairs

RISK LEVEL

TARGET: The entire office

Office Supplies

Letterhead

This prank works particularly well in tall office buildings. If your office is twenty floors or higher, this prank is a hoot and a half. Who will possibly get to the office first? Could **Old Timer** make it in a surprise win?

Get to work early and place a sign on the elevators that says they are Out of Order. This is most fun if the sign reads: DANGER: OUT OF ORDER. Even if the doors open, watch how many people refuse to get in and instead take the stairs. Wait until there's a good number of your coworkers trudging up the stairs and take the elevator up to greet them sympathetically.

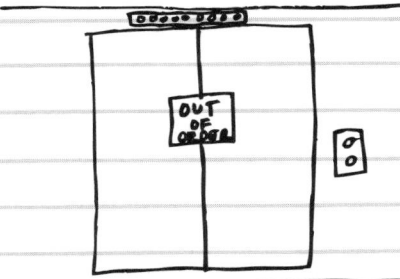

Spreading the News

TARGET: Talks Too Much

RISK LEVEL

Office Supplies

Computer

Finally, it's time to get back at **Talks Too Much** for all the time she wastes and the boring gossip she feels you need to know. While she's talking the ear off of yet another poor coworker, sneak into her office and change her e-mail defaults so they automatically BCC her boss or supervisor. Things will definitely get interesting when he gets to read all of her celebrity gossip and true-life relationship stories.

I Just Want to Bang on Me Drum All Day

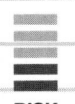

RISK LEVEL

TARGET: Idiot with All the Power

Office Supplies

Computer, a really awful and loud CD

This might be a more difficult task for you lazy middle managers. You who sneak out at 4:30 P.M. but insist you were there until 6 P.M. Yeah, you know who you are. In this case though, the extra time will be worth a tiny bit of effort.

Once **Idiot with All the Power** is out the door, stick the loudest, most obnoxious and even vile CD you can find into his computer (think Metallica, Nine Inch Nails, Marilyn Manson, or go for something dramatic by John Philips Sousa or Weird Al Yankovic). Make sure his music program is set to play automatically whenever a CD is inserted and crank the volume as loud as you can. Now shut it all down and head on home to bask in the glory of your own skills.

First thing in the morning, when **Idiot with All the Power** arrives at his desk, he's going to turn things on, and turn things up. The volume of the music coming from his computer is going to wake up more than just a few co-workers.

The Flaming Memo

RISK LEVEL

TARGET: Office Narc

Office Supplies

Computer

The perfect gag for **Office Narc**. The next time he's joyfully attending another painfully long meeting (at least that's what you would consider it), slip into his office and do an auto change on whatever document he was last working—hopefully it's a memo set to go out to the entire office.

For those of you who were promoted to middle management without any real skills, an auto change is a find and replace. Go through the document and have it automatically find the word "the" and change it to "shit"

or, better yet, substitue "dufus" for **"Office Narc."**

The smartest prankster will make the change clever and discreet so it won't be noticed when **Office Narc** does a quick glance at the document. For example, is **Office Narc's** real name Frank? Why not change it to Fu--? You get the idea.

Pest Control

RISK LEVEL

TARGET: Clock Watcher

Office Supplies

_As many plastic pests as you can find
at your local novelty shop_

When **Clock Watcher** leaves for the night—right on time as always!—sneak into his office and create an insect farm on his desk and all around the room. The truly brave middle management prankster will go to the local pet store and actually unload an ant farm (with a little sugar to keep them happy). For the prankster who wants to phone it in, rubber ants will do. (The occasional rubber rat adds a nice touch, too.) Get ready for some shrieks the next morning! Note: If you choose authenticity over impact, use the props sparingly and in less obvious locations.

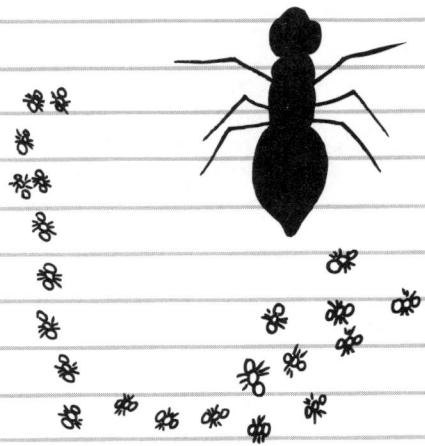

Surprise Party

RISK LEVEL

TARGET: Kisses the Boss's Ass

Office Supplies

Your finest threads

Around holiday time—or maybe close to **Idiot with All the Power's** birthday—pick a day and tell your office buddies to come in wearing their best party duds. No matter what the dress code is in your office, make sure everyone kicks it up a notch. When **Kisses the Boss's Ass** asks what the big occasion is, look at her quizzically. Say: "**Idiot with All the Power's** party is tonight. You didn't forget, did you?" Then gleefully watch your victim sweat and run back to his desk, scrambling to find the invitation that never came.

Wanted

Bodies (live ones!) needed for part-time positions in prestigious office park. Possible duties include: appreciative audience, partygoer (serious party duds a plus), office drone. Knowledge of law and flexibility to serve as witness in court preferable. Raucous laugh a must.

What's in a Name?

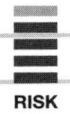

**RISK
LEVEL**

TARGET: Woeful Wallflower

Office Supplies

Computer

When **Woeful Wallflower** steps out for a meeting, make a quick dash for her computer. From her own e-mail account, send a companywide announcement proclaiming that she's officially changed her name. Accordingly, she'd like all coworkers to start addressing her as Ima Hobag or E. Z. Lay. Poor **Woeful Wallflower** will be mortified by all the new unwanted attention she receives! If your victim's a dude, assign him the moniker of Sam A. BinLaden or Harry Dickman.

Bumper Snickers

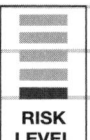

RISK LEVEL

TARGET: Nervous Nelly

Office Supplies

A few extra bucks

In your free time, surf the Web or browse your favorite novelty store to find the most obnoxious bumper stickers you can find. You've seen them on the road . . . "Danger: Fart Zone" and "Support Cannibalism: Eat Me." Buy a few and then wait for your chance.

When you have a free minute, make a quick dash outside and paste as many as you can to the back of **Nervous Nelly's** car. Chances are she won't even take notice when she leaves work that day and she'll go home offending every other driver on the road.

— CAT —
The OTHER white meat!

PRACTICE
SAFE SEX.
GO SCREW
YOURSELF!

Did Someone Forget the Potty?

RISK LEVEL

TARGET: Mr. Competitive

Office Supplies

Get to work a little early one morning and fill a large spray bottle with water. Sneak on over to **Mr. Competitive's** chair and douse it with water. Make sure to soak the cushion evenly so that it appears a uniform color. Then hide the dripping gun in a safe spot and wait for the drama to unfold.

After an ungentlemanly-like squeal, **Mr. Competitive** is sure to make a quick dash for the bathroom to survey the damage to his expensive threads.

Fast-track

If you **really** want to piss him off, leave a gift for him on his desk. His wet bottom will come back to a still-wet chair and an adult-sized diaper.

Jack-in-the-Box

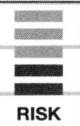

RISK LEVEL

TARGET: The first person through the door

Office Supplies

A very large box (perhaps a refrigerator box), a scary Halloween costume that includes a mask

Before work hours begin, don your creepy attire and place the large box in a highly trafficked hallway. Crawl inside. Now you just sit and wait . . . and probably sweat your pants off. It'll all be worth it, though, when your first unsuspecting victims stroll by. When you hear their footsteps falling very close to your hiding spot, jump out with a loud roar. Your coworkers will get the biggest scare of their lives.

Prank Pitfall

Warning! Try to avoid jumping out at any heart patients. You may end up with a lawsuit!

Sweet Charity

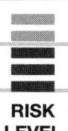

RISK LEVEL

TARGET: Idiot with All the Power

Office Supplies

The phone book/ Internet, phone

Sift through the yellow pages or browse the Internet for some worthy causes. Once you've found a few, give them a call pledging large sums of money . . . in **Idiot with All the Power's** name. Be sure to leave his address and office phone number for their all-important follow-up calls. When he gets the pledge card in the mail, he'll be overwhelmed by his own generosity!

THANK YOU
for
your pledge!

Playing with the Big Boys

RISK LEVEL

TARGET: Kisses the Boss's Ass

Office supplies

None

Poor **Kisses the Boss's Ass** desperately wants to become **Idiot with All the Power's** pet employee. He volunteers to pick up his dry cleaning and fetch him an afternoon coffee. It's time you tortured the pathetic weasel a little more.

Tell **Kisses the Boss's Ass** you're headed to **Idiot's** monthly poker game with the other uppity-ups in management. Get your buddy to say, "Yeah, I'm goin' too!" Convince the wannabe that he should meet up with you guys there—give him a phoney address. The poor schmuck will realize just how pathetic he is when he finds out he's been had.

Presentation Is Everything

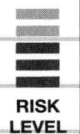

RISK LEVEL

TARGET: Mr. Competitive

Office Supplies

Access to the conference room

For weeks you've been listening to **Mr. Competitive** brag about the big company presentation he's been asked to run. Now his big day has arrived and nobody could be more excited . . . except maybe an expert prankster like yourself! After all, this meeting is ripe for sabotage.

A few minutes before the presentation is ready to begin, sneak into the empty conference room and switch around some slides or delete a few frames from his PowerPoint presentation.

When **Mr. Competitive** hits a snag in his program, it's likely to throw him off his game completely. Finally, he'll be eating some humble pie!

You're Fired!

RISK LEVEL

TARGET: Nervous Nelly

Office Supplies

None (but you'll need your bullshitting capabilities)

After regular business hours, when most employees—and especially the managers—have left for the day, stop by **Nervous Nelly's** desk and put on your most shock-stricken, sympathetic face.

Tell her: "Oh my gosh, I just heard! Are you okay?" She'll be completely perplexed. Tell her you have some extra boxes in your office if she'd like some help packing up her stuff. The panic is likely to set in now. She'll ask what you're talking about. Acting perplexed yourself, you'll explain that your friend in HR just told you **Nelly** had been "let go." With an uncomfortable smile, she'll say there must be some kind of a mistake. Hastily agree with her and then make a quick exit.

Poor **Nelly** will likely spend the night tossing and turning after being sure to update her résumé.

A Prankster Never Lays Off

RISK LEVEL

TARGET: He Who Knows Everything

Office Supplies

None (but you will need your supreme acting abilities)

Strike up a conversation with **He Who Knows Everything** one night at happy hour. Once there's a lull, say something like "So . . . things aren't looking good, huh?" He'll be utterly confused.

"You haven't heard?" you ask him, eyes wide. He'll shake his head.

"Word's going around of layoffs in the near future," you say.

He'll freak out and ask lots of questions, but all you can do is shrug and say that's what you've heard. If you have a friend assisting you on this one, you can nudge him and he can confirm the bad news.

He Who Knows Everything will spread the story like wildfire and soon the whole company will be surfing the classifieds.

A Picture of "Jon"

RISK LEVEL

TARGET: Nervous Nelly

Office Supplies

Digital camera

Using a digital camera, take a photo of one of the toilet stalls in the company restroom and download it to your work computer. When **Nervous Nelly** walks out of the bathroom and passes your desk, open the photo file and laugh hysterically. **Nervous Nelly** will see the photo on your computer and think you somehow rigged a video camera to watch her do her "business."

Delete the evidence immediately before you're arrested for being a perv!

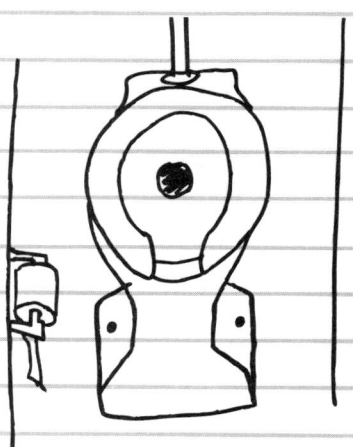

Lights Out!

RISK LEVEL

TARGET: Idiot with All the Power

Office Supplies

A phone, phone book

Times are tough, and stingy raises that don't even cover the rise in the cost of living sure don't help! Do you think the big-time muckity-mucks are having any trouble paying their bills? Not a chance!

Well, maybe you should give one of them the opportunity to see what it feels like to not make ends meet. Call your local electric company, posing as **Idiot with All the Power**, and tell them that you'll be moving to another state in a few weeks, so you're closing out your account and they can shut off the power on that date. Be sure to give them **Idiot's** address and congratulate yourself on scoring one for the "little man."

Up in Smoke

RISK LEVEL

TARGET: Everyone who uses the restroom

Office Supplies

Baby powder, paper

This trick only works for offices that have an automatic hand drier in the restroom. When you get a moment alone in the john, pull the bottle of baby powder out of your pocket and sprinkle as much of the stuff into the hand drier vent as possible. You may need to funnel it in by making a funnel with a piece of paper. It's a messy job, so be sure to clean up the extra residue before leaving the scene of the crime.

Hopefully, you have a cubicle near the bathroom exit, because you'll want to see the clouds of "smoke" following each person that walks out that door.

The Imaginary Intern

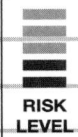

RISK LEVEL

TARGET: Clueless

Office Supplies

None (but you will need your bullshitting capabilities)

You've gotten word from your HR insiders that they finally filled the middle management position in your department. The new hire will get the office right next to **Clueless**.

On the eve of her first day, go have a chat with **Clueless** and give him the great "news": Your department is getting an intern and she starts tomorrow! The two of you will chat about all the busywork you can't wait to unload on her. The poor thing won't know what hit her.

On the new manager's first day, volunteer to introduce her around the department. Take her to meet **Clueless** being sure to use names only—not titles. When the new hire starts making herself at home in her new office, watch the smoke start to come out of **Clueless's** ears. When he comes complaining to you—"The intern gets the same office it took me five years to earn!!"—just shrug. As the day wears on and he starts unloading all of his grunt work on the "intern's" desk, their new business relationship will quickly begin to sour.

Once the truth finally comes out, it's **Clueless** that'll be doing all the extra work to make up for his mistake!

Client #9

RISK LEVEL

TARGET: Target: Stick Up Her Butt

Office Supplies

Local newspaper or computer, credit card

Stick Up Her Butt is such an easy target—it would be a shame to keep abusing her. But this one is just calling her name!

Find out the easiest way to put a classified ad in your local newspaper. You can probably put it together quickly on the paper's website. Have it read something like this: "Escort Service—Reasonable prices, sophisticated companions. We're completely at your disposal." Leave **Stick Up Her Butt's** first name and phone number for the contact information.

When the calls start pouring in, it's likely to be quite an education for dear **Stick Up Her Butt**!

Ew, Floaters!

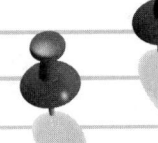

TARGET: The entire office

RISK LEVEL

Office Supplies

Many boxes of clear, unflavored gelatin

Make sure you pick up the right kind of gelatin at the supermarket. Just the plain old boring clear kind that's not flavored. Otherwise the tell-tale fruity aroma will be a dead giveaway.

Stay late one night and wait for everyone to go home. Make sure the cleaning staff has finished with the bathrooms for the evening. Go in and dump large amounts of the gelatin mix into all the toilets. You might want to find something like your boss's ruler, to stir the nasty concoction with. Now go home and let the gela-

tin set while all of your unsuspecting targets are sleeping peacefully.

The next morning your coworkers will enter the stalls, thinking nothing's amiss. The clear gelatin looks just like a bowl of toilet water. But no matter what their business, the waste will just float at the top of the bowl causing quite a scene and an even worse smell!

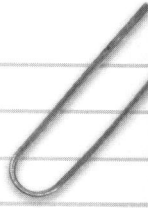

Toss at Your Own Risk

RISK LEVEL

TARGET: Everyone on staff

Office supplies

Computer, coworkers' printers

This is a great trick to play on the whole office, especially if they're a group of obedient team players. Create a document that reads "DO NOT DISCARD THIS SHEET" in very large letters. Print out enough copies for each printer in the office.

Get to work early and place a sheet in the output tray of every coworker's printer. They'll have no idea why it's there, but they're not likely to ask questions or recycle the silly message.

The Flipside of Cocky Living

RISK LEVEL

TARGET: He Who Thinks He's Prankproof (Ha!)

Office Supplies

None

By now, you've probably got a buddy who's been watching your shenanigans and feels perfectly secure thinking he knows all of your tricks. He's declared himself Prankproof. It's time you showed him that nobody's safe in this office!

Once your pal has left for the day, go over to his workspace and remove all of his desk drawers, leaving their contents in place. Remove everything on top of the desk. Computer, telephone, pen cup . . . *everything*! Otherwise, you'll have a real mess on your hands! Next, get your buddies to help you flip the desk upside down. Once it's resting on its top, insert the drawers back into the desk. Make sure they're securely closed. Now you guys can flip the desk back over and replace everything you removed from the desk top.

When your unsuspecting buddy comes in the next day, he'll go looking for a piece of paper, pull out the upside down drawer, and watch all of his office supplies fall to the floor! No drawers? No problem. Just leave the desk upside down—what a pain-in-the-ass way to start the day!

Do the Bathroom Shuffle

RISK LEVEL

TARGET: The entire office

Office Supplies

A few old pairs of pants and shoes, newspaper

Don't you just hate it when you really have to go, but all the bathroom stalls are occupied? Then you have to break into that little dance that we all know. Here's a prank that'll leave your whole office doing the bathroom shuffle.

Try to scrounge up as many pairs of old pants and shoes as there are stalls in the office restroom. Stuff the pants with newspaper and when just about everyone's left for the day, sneak into the bathroom with your stash.

Set up the pants and shoes to make it look as if all the stalls are occupied. When one of your poor uncomfortable victims comes in and does a quick check under the door, they'll see only the shoes and stuffed pants, and think they'll have to come back later.

It's up to you how long you want to keep this one up! This could get messy, folks!

You're All Wet

RISK LEVEL

TARGET: Anyone who rides the elevator

Office Supplies

A bucket, a tall stool or ladder (if available)

This is one of the oldest tricks in the book, but with a new spin. We've all heard the one where you balance the bucket of water on top of a doorway so that it falls on anyone who enters. Well, imagine how great it could work on elevator doors!

Fill up the bucket of water and move the stool or ladder in front of the elevator doors. Get the ladder as close to the doors as possible, then balance the bucket between the ladder and the center of the doors so that it's leaning on the crack of the doors, right where they open, ready to spill. Set up your camera and find a potted plant to hide behind, because you won't want to miss the deluge! The minute the doors open, it's occupants anxious to exit, the bucket will topple forward, right into the elevator, dousing everyone inside.

Company "Branding"

RISK LEVEL

TARGET: Mr. Competitive

Office Supplies

Credit card, computer

Mr. Competitive thinks he has the most company pride. It's time to show him up.

Do a search on the Internet for "custom temporary tattoo." Place an order for a washable tat of your company's logo. Once that baby gets mailed to you, apply it to a spot you don't mind showing off to your coworkers—some of you are probably more brazen than others. Then head into work the next morning, armed with your body art and the story of those awful needles and the exquisite pain.

Once **Mr. Competitive** gets a gander at that beauty, he'll likely be quite jealous. Encourage him to go out and get his own indelible ink!

Fast-track

To egg him on even more, give him a business card from one of the local tattoo parlors (make sure it's an especially skeevy one!).

Caution! Crime Scene

RISK LEVEL

TARGET: The criminals you work with

Office Supplies

Bright yellow caution tape, packing tape

Ever feel like you work with a bunch of derelicts? Chances are some of your coworkers feel that way too. So maybe this one won't come as such a shock to them . . .

Buy some bright yellow caution tape online or at your local hardware store. Then get to work very early one morning and wrap the tape around the entire perimeter of the property. Tape it onto all external doors and across all parking lot entrances.

Now go treat yourself to a donut at the local cops' favorite shop and feel like one of the gang.

Your coworkers will all be speculating about which one of them is the criminal and what crime has been perpetrated!

My Door's Always Open!

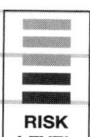

RISK LEVEL

TARGET: All elevator riders

Office Supplies
Piece of cardboard, tape

This one's sure to cause a traffic pileup in the elevator bank!

Get to work early and have a ladder or steady chair on hand. Carry it on over to the elevators with your small piece of cardboard and the tape. Push the elevator call button and quickly climb up. Holding onto the door, tape the piece of cardboard as close to the top as possible, so that it's not readily noticeable. Let the doors close, and then watch to see if they fall open once again. If you've positioned the cardboard properly, the doors should be obstructed enough that they just keep opening and closing.

The Falling Chair

RISK LEVEL

TARGET: Any of your office wet blankets

Office supplies

Office chair

This is a great trick to play on **Stick Up Her Butt**, **Kisses the Boss's Ass**, or **He Who Knows Everything**. In other words, all those office wet blankets you'd love to take down a peg (or chair) or two.

Wait until your coworker goes out to pick up lunch and enlist the help of a brave accomplice as lookout. Drop the coworker's chair to its lowest level. When she returns, engage the coworker's attention while she prepares to settle in with lunch. Then watch her drop to her chair . . . and keep on dropping! If injury occurs, make sure you check the numbers I've provided for cheap legal aid.

CYA

Blame maintenance for adjusting the chair height—" My chair did the SAME thing to me this morning. Weird!" (Wink, wink.)

A Bloody Good Idea

RISK LEVEL

TARGET: Nervous Nelly or Stick Up Her Butt

Office Supplies

Office water cooler

Ewww! This prank has a high gross-out factor, which is perfect for **Nervous Nelly** and **Stick Up Her Butt** in particular, but works for everyone in the office, which is what makes it brilliant.

There is always one person who changes the water cooler. If it's you, it's your lucky day. If it's not you, enlist the help of the person who usually does. Next time the water needs changing, add a few drops of red food coloring before setting it on the pedestal.

Actually, just go for it: Add a lot! About an hour later mention casually to someone that you cut your finger while changing the water.

Watch the color drain from your coworkers' faces! A great gross-out to liven up deadly office drudgery.

Because He's All That

TARGET: Mr. Competitive

RISK
LEVEL

Office Supplies

Photo of your victim, Photoshop or another graphic design program

The perfect prank for **Mr. Competitive** or anyone else who thinks he's all that. He wears too much cologne, saunters instead of walks, and sees nothing wrong with seating himself on the corner of your desk to regale you with stories of his latest conquests.

Well, isn't it time you made **Mr. Competitive** the poster boy he's always wanted to be? You might need to enlist the help of your creative accomplice, but use a little graphic design expertise and create a beautifully detailed poster featuring **Mr. Competitive** as the new face of . . . herpes? genital warts? a shoplifter? a meth addict? Pick the disease of the day or the problem of your choice. Make it as libelous as you want or make it simple. Could he be the face of an overeater? Or what about the face of a bed wetter or the face of a lunch thief?

Once you've chosen your poster style and graphic, hang them throughout the office. In the elevators, bathrooms, and conference rooms. **Mr. Competitive** will have to work hard to find and remove all the posters, and if you're really smart you might even consider the bulletin board in the local Starbucks. Why not make this a global prank campaign?

Master Ball Buster

RISK LEVEL

TARGET: Mr. Competitive

Office Supplies

Credit card, tape

You and **Mr. Competitive** have had a running argument about the best team in baseball. You're a Yankees man and he's a rude Red Sox lover. Now's the time to kick that rivalry up a notch.

Take a trip to your local sports novelty shop and find every piece of Yankees décor you can get your hands on. The louder and bolder, the better!

Get to work early the next day and get a friend and fellow pinstripes fan to help you flood **Mr. Competitive's** office with blue and white.

When your victim finds what you've left waiting for him, he's bound to know the culprit. That's okay. It was all worth it. You scored a homerun!

Cha-Cha-Cha-Chia

RISK LEVEL

TARGET: He Who Knows Everything

Office Supplies

Watercress seeds, cotton, your victim's keyboard

This prank is perfect for **He Who Knows Everything**, since he's an expert in ALL topics, including animals, plants, and life-and-death matters.

Head to the garden store to get yourself a small packet of watercress seeds and swing by the bathroom for a few cotton balls. Wait until **He Who Knows Everything** leaves for a long weekend or short vacation. Because of growing time, you'll need to get access to his keyboard early on in his absence. As I see it, you have two options here. The first, for those just getting out of Entry Level, you should get your hands on an old, unusable keyboard and simply replace **Knows Everything's** with this "new" equipment. But for those willing to chance a little more than simply a summons from the boss, I say just use the keyboard **He Who Knows Everything** already has on his desk.

Once you have access to the keyboard, remove some of the key tabs and line the underside with cotton—thin strips that fit between the keys are perfect. The cotton will hold not only the water, but also the seeds and supply perfect growing space for your watercress. Once your cotton is in place, liberally spray it with mists of water and return the keys to their position, or something moderately resembling their position. And then add seeds. You'll want to make sure the seeds slip in between the cracks of the keys and don't sit on top. If they sit on top, they probably won't grow.

Each day during **He Who Knows Everything's** absence, swing by with your spray bottle to keep those seeds moist. It won't take but a matter of days before **he** has a nice lush garden to call his own.

Dear Dumbass

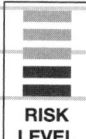

RISK LEVEL

TARGET: Kisses the Boss's Ass

Office Supplies

Computer

A variation of The Flaming Memo, but even better. When **Kisses the Boss's Ass** is busy doing what he does best, slip into his office and go to Auto Correct under Tools on his word processing program. Set the program to automatically replace his full name with "Dumbass" or "Ass Kisser." Watch the fun with each memo **Kisses the Boss's Ass** sends.

What Did You Say?

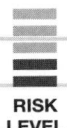

RISK LEVEL

TARGET: Anyone with a voice dictation program

Office Supplies

A voice dictation program

Since this prank works only for those with a voice dictation program, you won't have much choice when it comes to your victims. (A voice dictation program types what you say so you don't have to use a keyboard.) Most people who have it on their computer don't even know they have it, which makes this prank extra sinister.

Select your unwitting victim. If you have a choice, I recommend **Clueless, Talks Too Much, Caffeine Freak,** and especially **Kisses the Boss's Ass.** Any arrogant or clueless coworker will work just fine. Sneak into the victim's office and activate the dictation program. Whenever your victim is chatting in his office, the computer will try to type what he is saying. And if the office worker is highly strung, well, let's just say it just might make your day to watch the fireworks that ensue while your frustrated friend tries to regain control of his computer.

Posting Your Decorating Ideas

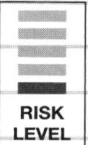

RISK LEVEL

TARGET: Naps at His Desk

Office Supplies

Hundreds of Post-it notes

While this prank is unlikely to get you into too much trouble it is time-consuming and will take some strategic planning. The goal? To wallpaper **Naps at His Desk's** entire office with Post-it notes.

The only thing you really need to do is plan for a time when **Naps at His Desk** is heading out early and then get to work. With a Post-it pad in hand and as much help as you can get, your goal is to cover as much surface area as possible before you can't take it anymore. Of course you want to get his computer, desk, walls and chair, but don't forget the ceiling, floor, door, and even the shoes he leaves for emergency situations. The more you cover, the more impressive the prank. And don't forget to throw in a little pink and blue for fun. Remember wallpaper should never be just all yellow.

WIDGET/TEX PERSONNEL FILE
PERSONAL AND CONFIDENTIAL

Date: *January 2*

Employee Full Name: *Naps at His Desk*

Position: *Information Technology Lackey*

Supervisor: *Geek Extraordinaire*

Payroll: *Docking next check for 12 hours of stolen company time*

Performance Appraisals: *Employee seemed uninterested during review process, yawning throughout the session. Coworkers have complained that he is not returning calls for tech support. Office productivity is down due to computer problems going unchecked.*

Report History: *Mailroom clerk filed a complaint after she attempted to deliver package and found employee unconscious on the floor. After calling 911, she heard snoring and realized he was asleep and not suffering from a medical emergency.*

Status: *Red flagged. Employee has received his first official warning.*

Résumé Ripoff

RISK LEVEL

TARGET: Conspiracy Theorist and Nervous Nelly

Office Supplies

Computer (with Internet access)

Want a great way to play with the heads of both **Conspiracy Theorist** and **Nervous Nelly**?

Get an electronic copy of your victim's résumé. A pranking cohort in HR can be uber-helpful in this instance. But don't worry if you can't get your hands on an actual résumé—feel free to make it up! (Master Pranksters are creative and resourceful, after all.) Log on to as many of the online job sites that you can. Set up an account on each in your coworker's name. Follow the individual online directions to upload the résumé file.

Sit back and enjoy the chaos as **Conspiracy Theorist's** phone starts ringing with unexpected job offers.

We Can't Afford Mistakes

RISK LEVEL

TARGET: Forever an Assistant or Kisses the Boss's Ass

Office Supplies

Access to coworker's phone

This is a great prank to play on **Forever an Assistant** or **Kisses the Boss's Ass**, who can't tolerate or afford making mistakes. While your victim is out to lunch, hide her phone in her office somewhere. When she returns, tell your victim in passing that the Biggest Client is calling in to talk to her. (It also works to leave her a note saying **Idiot with All the Power** called and would call back after lunch.) It's time to enlist the help of your Creative Accomplice. Have the CA immediately call the victim's phone. Watch as she runs around the office trying to find it before the ringing stops!

I Ain't No Limburger

RISK LEVEL

TARGET: Stick Up Her Butt

Office supplies

Stinky cheese

Any prank that involves stinky cheese has to be good. I highly recommend (from years of experience) either of the following pungent cheeses: limburger (oy vey!) and Stilton (whew!).

First order of business: Purchase the stinky cheese.

Second on the agenda: Hide the stinky cheese in your coworker's office. This is the perfect prank for (need I say it?) **Stick Up Her Butt.** For a little variety, on another day, you can try hiding the cheese in the conference room before a big meeting. Sit down next to **Old Timer,** sniff a few times, and move quickly away. Works like a charm to undermine someone's sense of security before a presentation too. Downright diabolical!

A Call from on High

RISK LEVEL

TARGET: Talks Too Much

Office Supplies

Coworker's cell phone

Calling all sneaky pranksters! You'll have to use your cat burglar skills to get a hold of your unsuspecting coworker's cell phone while she is out of the office. Use the help of a creative accomplice to watch out while you secure the cell phone. You'll have to work fast to pull this off! Get your hands on a ladder or sturdy chair and hide the phone in the ceiling tiles above your victim's desk. This is highly recommended for **Talks Too Much**, whose phone is sure to ring on cue.

Prank Pitfall

Make sure the cell phone battery has a strong charge, otherwise, all your effort may be for naught. (With the amount of yapping Talks Too Much does, her battery is always dead!)

Pick Up the Damn Phone

RISK LEVEL

TARGET: Woeful Wallflower

Office Supplies

Coworker's cell phone

This is a good trick for **Woeful Wallflower**. Steal into her office and grab her cell phone when she's not looking. You might want to enlist the support of a creative accomplice to get her out of the office for a while. Change her ring tone to something really offensive and obnoxious, like Crazy Bitch, Baby's Got Back, or pretty much anything from *South Park*. Then hide her phone in her office and keep calling her!

Santa's Little Secret

RISK LEVEL

TARGET: Woeful Wallflower, Stick Up Her Butt, or Sleeps Her Way to the Top

Office Supplies

Basket, paper

Tell your coworker (see recommended list of victims, below) that the office is pulling names for a Secret Santa gift exchange. Fill a basket (a bag will also work) with slips of paper that all contain the name of your target's least favorite officemate. She'll pull the one and only name, and you can then sit back and watch when she bestows her unsuspecting nemesis with a gift and receives nothing but a lot of frowns and paranoid glances in return.

Recommended for: **Woeful Wallflower, Stick Up Her Butt,** and **Sleeps Her Way to the Top.**

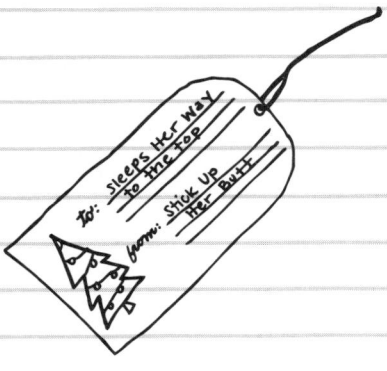

The Ax Is About to Fall

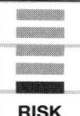

RISK LEVEL

TARGET: Conspiracy Theorist

Office Supplies

None

Enlist your nonwork prank-ster friends (and I'm sure you have a lot of them, right?) for this tricky mission. Give each of your friends the office phone number of **Conspiracy Theorist** or another paranoid coworker. Have them call your coworker and inquire about the opening for his position. Poor guy will think the end is coming!

Fast-track

Get your hands on your victim's cell phone number and have your friends prank call him on weekends, evenings, and especially during the middle of the night!

Kiss My Job Goodbye

RISK LEVEL

TARGET: Idiot with All the Power

Office Supplies

Company copy machine

Idiot with All the Power definitely needs to be taken down a notch or two. When you know he's going to be using the copier for an important memo or report (or making **Forever an Assistant** do it for him), replace all the paper with paper that says "Kiss My Ass" in small type at the bottom of the page.

There's No Such Thing as a Free Lunch

RISK LEVEL

TARGET: Mooch

Office supplies

Access to your coworker's lunch

Mooch has met his match with you. When he's out of his cubicle, steal in and take his lunch for a nice noontime meal for yourself. Make sure you leave him an IOU.

MOOCH'S LUNCH

Fast-track

If you're feeling especially gutsy, clean out an entire day's worth of lunches from the fridge, and watch the confusion and listen for growling stomachs.

Shrine On!

RISK LEVEL

TARGET: Sleeps Her Way to the Top

Office Supplies

Photo of the boss, candle, object from boss's office, flowers

When **Sleeps Her Way to the Top** is out of her office enlist the help of a crafty lookout and sneak into her office with your bag of tricks. Set up a shrine in a corner of her office with the picture of the Big Boss Man, some objects from his office, a candle, flowers, and any other crazy items you can collect.

Go the extra mile and see if you can come up with a pretense to get the boss to go into her office before she returns. Holy creep out!

Model Family

RISK LEVEL

TARGET: Stick Up Her Butt or Mr. Competitive

Office Supplies

Magazine cutouts of less than attractive people

Your prime victims for this sneaky stunt would be someone with an inflamed ego, so of course, **Stick Up Her Butt** or **Mr. Competitive** immediately come to mind!

Sneak into your victim's office and replace any photographs with magazine cutouts of less than attractive people. Feel free to blacken teeth and add horns. Be creative.

Kids Say the Darndest Things

RISK LEVEL

TARGET: He Who Knows Everything or Office Narc

Office Supplies

Paper

Create speaking bubbles for your target's family photos, such as "You should be fired!" "Sleeps in wife's nightgown." Sneak into **He Who Knows Everything's** office or **Office Narc's** cube, tape 'em on and sit back as hilarity ensues.

It's also fun to try to do this while **Naps at His Desk** is in there napping. Up the ante why don't you?

You're terrible in bed!

CYA

Blame the boss's pre-teenager, you know, the punk who visited the office just last week? What took you so long to see it, eh?

Happy Birthday to ME

RISK LEVEL

TARGET: Anyone in need of a good prank

Office Supplies

Pen

Of course, this might not even qualify as a prank: It's just good common sense. After all, you are the most popular person (not!) in the office because of your great gift for pranking. So, why not sneak into your coworkers' offices and write your birthday on their calendars?

Make sure you also write it a week or two ahead so they have enough time to get you presents. I wrote something like this: "Don't forget Mae's birthday next Wednesday."

Then two days later: "Must buy Mae gift." Then: "Organize Mae's party!"

Who knows, maybe something will stick! Make sure to target everyone in the office for maximum loot.

Prank Pitfall

Be on guard that day, as your coworkers might take the opportunity on this special day to pull a big prank on you, in which case you might end up eating a big piece of humble pie if you're not careful!

It's All about Me

RISK LEVEL

TARGET: anyone who happens to think he (or she) is all that

Office Supplies

Access to coworker's photo, Scotch tape

The more believable this prank is, the funnier it will be, so make sure your target thinks quite a lot of herself, like **Stick Up Her Butt**, **He Who Knows Everything**, or **Idiot with All the Power**.

Steal a picture of your victim from his office. Make color copies and write "It's My Birthday" at the bottom in big letters. Plaster all over the office.

IT'S MY BIRTHDAY!

Did I Do Something?

RISK LEVEL

TARGET: Nervous Nelly

Office Supplies

Yellow police tape

Get into work early one day and place yellow police tape over your victim's cubicle. Works really well with **Nervous Nelly**, who might actually believe she did something wrong.

CYA

Blame the rent-a-cop security team—" They must have been working overtime last night!"

When I Was Your Age, I Walked Uphill Both Ways

RISK LEVEL

TARGET: Old Timer

Office Supplies

Orange safety cone

Get into work early one day and place an orange safety cone in your victim's usual parking spot. Works well with **Old Timer**—whose parking spot is probably the closest to the door. When he is forced to park farther away and walk, you're really just doing a public service. Exercise keeps him young!

Let Your Fingers Do the Freaking Out

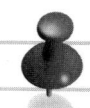

RISK LEVEL

TARGET: Stick Up Her Butt

Office Supplies

None

Here's another quick trick for a lazy afternoon. Slip into **Stick Up Her Butt's** office during lunch or before work. Mix up her Rolodex so that it's hopelessly de-alphabetized. Go to town: You'll love watching her freak out as she has to meticulously reorganize it ASAP!

CYA

Blame the Frightened Intern, whom you overheard saying he needed to find the Big Client's number per the Big Boss Man.

Hey, Handsome!

TARGET: Clueless

RISK LEVEL

Office Supplies

Computer

Face it, you're beautiful. And you should feel free to share that beauty with others, right? Well, here's your opportunity. This works best on **Clueless** as he has no idea how to fix things, and besides, this prank only gets maximum bang for the buck if it's not fixed immediately.

Download a picture of yourself onto a disk or flash drive. Sneak into your coworker's office during lunch while he's out (don't forget to have your crafty accomplice act as lookout!). Insert the disk. Change the computer screen saver and upload your picture in its place. Hey, handsome!

Is That a Gun in Your Pocket?

RISK LEVEL

TARGET: He Who Knows Everything or Mr. Competitive

Office Supplies

None

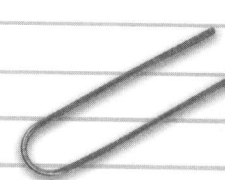

Here's one for the truly mean-spirited. This is a satisfying prank to play on **He Who Knows Everything** or **Mr. Competitive**.

When you know your co-worker is in the middle of giving a presentation he has worked hard to put together, call his cell phone or text him to tell him he's doing a terrible job. Or better yet, sit in the audience in front and keep nodding at his fly with your chin to really throw him off. He'll think he's hanging out for the world to see and it will definitely throw him off his game. Touché!

Yellow Peril

TARGET: The Hypochondriac

RISK LEVEL

Office Supplies

Yellow food dye, the office water cooler, paper

Halfway through a slow day, after your coworkers have wet their whistles several times, put some yellow dye in the water cooler so it turns a scary shade not to be found naturally. Hang a sign on the water cooler that says: WATER COOLER CONTAM- INATED and sit back while panic ensues. Keep your eye on **The Hypochondriac** for sure, as she's sure to have a meltdown!

Getting to Know Each Other

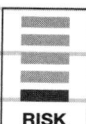

RISK LEVEL

TARGET: Everyone

Office supplies

Paper

Some days you just need some privacy. Take advantage of your status as Master Prankster to create your own.

Using your computer, create an "offical" looking sign that says: OUT OF ORDER: PLEASE USE THE WOMEN'S ROOM [or MEN'S ROOM] and hang it on the door. Enjoy your privacy and listen for screams of surprise from down the hall.

Foiled Again!

RISK LEVEL

TARGET: Office Narc

Office Supplies

A case of tinfoil

While this prank isn't particularly harmful, it is time-consuming, both for you and your victim, and could cause a few hard feelings. Perfect for just about anyone—I of course love to use this on **Office Narc.**

Plan this prank on a night when you can easily convince others you have good reason to stay late and plan on staying very, very late. In fact, if I were you, I would gather my accomplices, pick up a twelve-pack of beer, order pizza, and plan to be tired the next day.

As soon as the office is clear it's time to whip out the beer and get to work. Your task? To wrap each individual item in **Office Narc's** office with foil. That means the stapler, photos of his kids, his pens, his desk, his chair . . . well, you get the picture. By the time he walks into work the next day **Office Narc's** cubicle should be shiny, bright, and beautiful.

Keep It Clean

RISK LEVEL

TARGET: Stick Up Her Butt

Office Supplies

Letterhead

Office memos are a prank-ster's bread and butter, and while you'll come across quite a few different versions, this is one of my all-time favorites.

Perfect for **Stick Up Her Butt,** this prank will keep everyone howling for days. Grab a piece of letterhead or, if you wish, hop on **Idiot with All the Power's** computer one day while he's lunching at the fast-food joint. Create an office-wide memo demanding **Stick Up Her Butt** cease and desist from washing her undergarments in the bathroom sink.

For those who might want to take this prank to the next level, this version is even a little more fun, at least in my humble, but expert, opinion. Don't target anyone specifically in the memo, but instead send around an anonymous memo asking that whoever is washing and drying her undergarments in the women's room please stop. It's gross. And then plant a few pieces of raunchy and dirty underwear around the women's room.

Naked Fridays

RISK LEVEL

TARGET: Kisses the Boss's Ass

Office Supplies

Letterhead

Friends who work at home often tell me about the joys of Naked Fridays. The day where they can sit around in their skivvies (or bare-assed) and answer e-mail and take conference calls without ever needing to wonder if their socks match or worry that zippers will pop. Of course, I imagine there are other things to worry about when working naked, but since I'm just another office schlub it's not my problem.

It's unlikely you'll be able to convince anyone to actually come to work naked, but it is possible you can convince someone to come in wearing less-than-appropriate clothing. Early in the week, send around a memo to just one person, preferably **Kisses the Boss's Ass.** The memo should be "from" **Idiot with All the Power** and should be informing "everyone" that from now on your very corporate, suit-wearing office is going business casual on Fridays; khakis and even jeans are now acceptable.

Slippery When Wet

RISK LEVEL

TARGET: The Hypochondriac

Office Supplies

Bathroom hand soap, a container of lubricant

Gross! There is no better word to describe this prank and what everyone will be thinking when they go to wash their hands. Instead of getting delicious smelling foamy soap, they get a handful of sticky, slippery, gross lubricant. **The Hypochondriac** will find it particularly offensive!

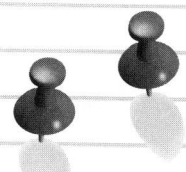

The Three-Martini Lunch

RISK LEVEL

TARGET: Old Timer

Office Supplies

Letterhead

What happened to those days when men were men and everyone had a cocktail at their desk? Sadly we've all become a bunch of working stiffs, and it's time to lighten things up! This is exactly what you're going to tell **Old Timer** when you let him know that tomorrow's client meeting in the office is with a big drinker and **Idiot with All the Power** has asked that we supply him with a lavish bar to keep him happy. Tell **Old Timer** it's his job to stock that bar using his company credit card. If you're lucky, **Idiot with All the Power** will find the only way to get over the embarrassment is for everyone to have a drink, or five.

Daylight Savings

RISK LEVEL

TARGET: Kisses the Boss's Ass

Office Supplies

Computer, office clocks

While you can't deny that more sunlight is a true benefit of Daylight Savings Time, in my mind the loss of an hour of sleep kills me every year. I swear, it takes me months to catch up. But I digress.

There's nobody who can benefit from this prank more than **Kisses the Boss's Ass**. I am so sick of his righteous ways and sucking up, and I'm really sick of hearing about his perfect lifetime attendance record. Are you really telling me this guy has never missed a day of anything? Well, it's time for that to change.

When you get the chance, slip into **Kisses the Boss's Ass's** office and change all of his clocks; those on his computer, on the wall, every clock you can get your hands on should be moved one hour ahead. Then, the next day, go back in and change all of his clocks an hour behind (the actual time). Keep this up for a week and see how long it takes this Office brown-noser to catch on to what's happening. As soon as he does, set all the clocks to the right time. I will guarantee he'll be late to almost everything that week.

Technology Will Kill You

RISK LEVEL

TARGET: Conspiracy Theorist

Office Supplies

Computer

Nothing rattles an office more than phone problems. Okay, maybe computer problems have a bigger impact, but phone problems are definitely a close second.

Using the boss's assistant's e-mail account, send out an urgent, high-priority company-wide e-mail informing everyone that the phone company just called and there are serious and dangerous problems with the phone system. Use could result in electrocution. To avoid being zapped, any employee using the phone should keep their feet off the floor until the call has ended. So, how do you make this work? Send out the e-mail in the middle of **Conspiracy Theorist's** most important sales call of the year.

Party Time!

RISK LEVEL

TARGET: Idiot with All the Power

Office Supplies

Empty box, shredded paper, or confetti from a hole punch

Take an empty box and fill it up with shredded paper and hole-punch confetti. ~~Fill it to the top.~~ And then just before **Idiot with All the Power's** very important meeting in the conference room, slip the box onto the middle of the table, top side down. As the clients come in and sit down, **Idiot with All the Power** will see the offending box and reach to pick it up. Imagine the mayhem as confetti rains down on his biggest client's head.

America's Next Top Porn Star

TARGET: Stick Up Her Butt

RISK LEVEL

Office Supplies   _A collection of porn (preferably worn looking with very racy covers)_

While this is incredibly simple to pull off, today's sexual harassment policies mean the prank carries a lot of potential for trouble. And obviously your perfect target is going to be **Stick Up Her Butt**. Really there's no one better.

Arrive early at work one day (or set up the prank before leaving the day before) and set your stack of "dirty movies" on **Stick Up Her Butt's** desk with a note that simply says, "You were right! Thanks!"

Watch the fun, the horror, and the chaos that results, especially if you were wise enough to choose a day when **Stick Up Her Butt** is late coming into the office and the potential of someone else seeing them is high.

Pave It Forward

RISK LEVEL

TARGET: The entire office

Office Supplies

Letterhead

This simple trick works well if you plan it for what's scheduled to be a sweltering hot day. Send around a memo announcing that tomorrow the parking lot is going to be repaved and because of that everyone is going to need to park at the building next door—or maybe down the block or maybe have them fight it out for street spaces? I'll leave that decision up to you.

To get true enjoyment out of this prank I would suggest you plan on getting to work early, but into the office late. Take your Venti-Triple-Shot- Nonfat-Latte and low-fat scone and settle in to a parking spot just outside of the building. A space not in the parking lot, but one that gives you a bird's-eye view of everyone trekking down the street into the office. You'll be amazed by how irritated people can get by just a little exercise. And then, once everyone is quietly at their desks, pull into the primo spot right next to the door and waltz in to work.

Working for Peanuts

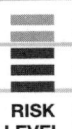

RISK LEVEL

TARGET: Office Narc or He Who Knows Everything

Office supplies

Boxes and boxes of packing peanuts, packing tape

Similar to Foiled Again, this is a great prank for **Office Narc** or maybe even **He Who Knows Everything**. The advantage is that this trick is a little less time-consuming, although still not for the faint of heart.

Your task here is to acquire boxes, bags and bins of packing peanuts. (Here's where your connections in the mailroom come in handy.)

Once you've got your peanuts, grab your accomplice, plan on staying past the closing bell, order some pizza and pick up a six-pack. (After all, if you're going to be at the office late, you might as well make a party out of it!)

The minute the coast is clear, gather your packing peanuts, rolls of packing tape and maybe even a box or two and get to work. The really hearty prankster will tape up that cubicle door (to keep the peanuts from flying out) and start dumping. Pull up chair and let the peanuts rain down into **He Who Knows Everything's** domain. For extra fun you might want to open his desk drawers before the drop begins.

Debbie Does the Office

RISK LEVEL

TARGET: Office Narc

Office Supplies

Computer

This prank is for the truly ballsy prankster. Have the number for unemployment ready just in case.

Wait until **Office Narc** is out at lunch and tiptoe into his office. Change his computer home page to a porn site. This works particularly well if your coworker has a cubicle in the hallway. But get out of the way ASAP!

99 Luft Balloons

RISK LEVEL

TARGET: Hot Temp

Office Supplies

Helium tank, lots of balloons

Here's another prank that works for the entire office, but if you're up for the challenge, if you'd like to keep things small and intimate, try this on **Hot Temp**, the girly-girl of the office who needs to be noticed at all times. She's the one who freaks out if no one notices her expensive new haircut or the polish on her nails. Well, this is a prank that is sure to get her lots of attention.

All you need to get started are a helium tank, bags and bags of balloons, and time alone in the office. Once you have all three get that air flowing and fill those balloons. Then fill her office. **Hot Temp** will certainly get the attention she needs when she shows up the next day to an office full of balloons.

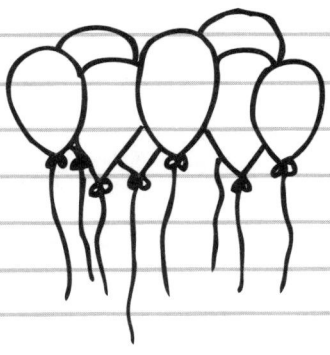

Needed: Office Grunt

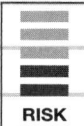

RISK LEVEL

TARGET: Forever an Assistant

Office Supplies

Money for a classified ad

The only real challenge about this prank is that it's not cheap. Have you ever looked at the price of a classified ad? Crazy how expensive they are. But remember, a good prank has no price. So fork over the dough, or take up a collection. It might be nice to bring a few of your coworkers in on the act for a change.

Once you have money in hand (cash ONLY), head down to the local newspaper and place an ad for **Forever an Assistant's** job. Let everyone know that **Idiot with All the Power** is seeking a full-time assistant to handle all the very important grunt work **Forever an Assistant** handles. And then, that morning, drop the paper with the ad on her desk with a Post-it letting her know that if she's looking for a job, you think you've found the perfect one. Just before the resumes start pouring in, watch as she panics with confusion.

Gone Fishin'

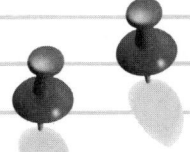

TARGET: Stick Up Her Butt

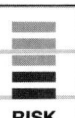

RISK LEVEL

Office Supplies

Ultrathin fishing line

This prank is perfect for **Stick Up Her Butt**, or anyone else who freaks out if someone touches even a pen on his desk.

The first thing you'll need is full access to **Stick Up Her Butt's** desk for at least twenty minutes. Try it when everyone else is at a meeting, lunch, or even at the end of the day so she'll come in to a fun morning treat. Take your fishing line and carefully tie it to a number of light things on the desk—the mouse, pencils, or tape it to the back of a notepad. And don't forget the phone receiver. This is an especially important one. Then string all of your line down under the desk to the chair. Push **Stick Up Her Butt's** chair in as far as you can and tie all the fish line to the front at the bottom. And before leaving check the desk so that line is as transparent as possible. You don't want **Stick Up Her Butt** to discover what you've been up to before you even have a chance to enjoy the fun.

And then watch things fly, literally, when the desk chair is pulled out.

Showing Off the Family

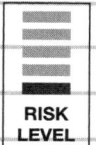

RISK LEVEL

TARGET: Clock Watcher

Office Supplies

a photo editing program, family photos from your victim's office

This is a project that's going to take some time, so I would recommend dedicating a weekend to the job or planning it for when **Clock Watcher** is out enjoying every minute of that fancy vacation with his perfect kids, beautiful wife, and well-trained dog.

Your first task will be to steal all the family photos from his office; the framed photos, those tucked into the corner of his computer and the ones tacked to his bulletin board—you know, the ones of his wife in a bikini and his perfectly tanned,

well-behaved kids (yeah right).

The real fun begins once you have the photos in hand! First, scan them all into your computer. For those with minimal photo-editing skills I would simply advise replacing the heads of the family with those of animals, other office coworkers, or even yourself (but remember, that incriminates you). For those with more talent, go for the big guns: replace T-shirts with more explicit phrases, increase appendage size, or simply add buck teeth, orange hair, or other unflattering looks to the family.

Then, before **Clock Watcher** returns from his "fabulous vacation" at 9:00 A.M. the next morning (and not a moment before), you can put the edited photos back in place. Your first task is to see how long it takes before he notices, and your next task is enjoy his reaction when he does. Give him about a week to stew and then sneak in and return all the original photos as if nothing happened.

WIDGET/TEX PERSONNEL FILE
PERSONAL AND CONFIDENTIAL

Date: *June 15*

Employee Full Name: *Clock Watcher*

Position: *Data Entry Specialist*

Supervisor: *Idiot with All the Power*

Payroll: *Remains at entry-level pay until next review*

Performance Appraisals: *Due to high work volume, superior has offered to pay employee time and a half for overtime, but employee has declined. While employee is incredibly punctual in the mornings, he often leaves work on his desk at the end of the day in order to get out at exactly 5:00 P.M.*

Report History: *Previous review was performed at end of day and superior reported that employee got up and left midsentence.*

Bubble, Bubble, Toil, and Trouble

RISK LEVEL

TARGET: The entire office

Office Supplies

A bottle of super-sudsy dish soap

If you work in an office with regular toilets, you know, the kind you find in your home with tanks and not the industrial type with a big pipe that leads to nowhere, you're in luck. This isn't a prank for anyone in particular, but really for your own enjoyment and amusement.

When you know the coast is clear, sneak into the bathroom with your extra large bottle of dish soap. In this case you'll want to buy the expensive kind, a kind that really bubbles up and holds its bubbles. I happen to be a fan of Ivory, but I'll leave the brand choice to you.

Get yourself into a stall and dump the entire bottle of soap into the tank, exit (don't you dare flush), and wait for your victim. I wouldn't recommend sitting around in the bathroom to wait, that will make people a little nervous in all sorts of other ways, but instead, watch from a key vantage point and give your victim about five minutes before wandering in. The fun will begin with the next flush, when loads of bubbles come pouring from the toilet.

You've Got Mail

TARGET: Naps At His Desk

RISK
LEVEL

Office Supplies

Computer

While not a difficult prank to pull off, this one will undoubtedly anger more than a few people—your victim, your boss, and definitely the guys in IT.

You'll want to undertake this prank when **Naps at His Desk** is away, but not gone for too long. If he's at a long meeting, lunch, or snoozing in the car he's going to miss half the excitement. When he's run to the bathroom or taking a snack break, slip into his chair, pull up his e-mail program, and highlight (select all) every e-mail in his in-box. And then simply hit "open." If he's like most of us, it's unlikely he's cleaned out an e-mail since he started the job . . . ten years ago. Just imagine how much time it will take to open thousands and thousands of e-mails. And the beauty of it is that even if he shuts down the computer it's very likely it will restart exactly where he left off, trying to open thousands of e-mails. Unless he gets someone else in there to help, it will take hours before he can get back to work.

Cleaning Day

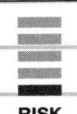

RISK LEVEL

TARGET: Kisses the Boss's Ass

Office Supplies

Letterhead

This little prank is absolutely perfect for **Kisses the Boss's Ass.** The next time you know he's getting ready for a big meeting, maybe even the one with your biggest client, it's time to set things right and finally put him in his place.

The day before the big meeting send **Kisses the Boss's Ass** a memo announcing the meeting has been canceled. Don't be afraid to really talk things up. Let "everyone" know that the client has decided the meeting isn't necessary. They are so happy with your company that they are planning on moving forward as hoped. As an added bonus to this great news, **Idiot with All the Power** is letting everyone sleep in late. Ironically no one is required to come in to the office until the time the meeting was "originally" scheduled for. And please wear your grungiest cleaning clothes because **Idiot with All the Power** is ordering lunch, beer, and snacks and calling it office cleaning day. Instead of the big meeting, the plan is to shut things down and scrub house.

Fries with That?

RISK LEVEL

TARGET: Mr. Competitive

Office Supplies

Pen, set of wheels

Mr. Competitive is pretty proud of his position in the company and is always looking for an easy way to get that next promotion. But how would he fare at a minimum-wage job?

Take a weekend afternoon to drive by a few fast-food restaurants, supermarkets, and discount chain stores. Pick up an application from each spot and fill it out using **Mr. Competitive's** name and contact information. Maybe Wal-Mart is looking for a new greeter, and your victim will find his new calling!

Putting Your Cups in a Row

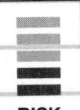

RISK LEVEL

TARGET: Stick Up Her Butt

Office Supplies

Paper water cups, water, a stapler

Stick Up Her Butt likes perfection in everything she does. Her hair is never out of place, she's never had a stain on her clothes, and her desk is clean and in perfect condition at the end of every day.

You'll need to arrive to work a little early to pull this off, or, for those of you who can't imagine putting in even an extra three minutes at your desk, this is a good lunchtime activity. Fill at least ten cups with water. Be generous and fill them as full as you dare. Then line them up on **Stick Up Her Butt's** desk. Feel free to get creative if you want. The cups could easily be placed in a straight line from one edge of the desk to the other, or you could create a circle, or maybe a flower? Channel the artist in you and do whatever you have time for. Once all the cups are in place, get out your stapler and staple all of them together. Now watch **Stick Up Her Butt** try to remove them without causing the great flood.

Executive Idiocy

Only top-level executives are ready for these sneaky stunts.

These are pranks that will take a little time but are guaranteed to give the biggest reward (or cause the most damage).

You're the big guy now. Or at least you think you are. You wear the fancy suits, sit in the corner office, and boss almost everyone else around. But do you really think you're an executive prankster? Here's your test. Let's see if you can hack it.

Flower Power

RISK LEVEL

TARGET: Sleeps Her Way to the Top

Office Supplies

Telephone, Yellow Pages, a little cash

Nothing gets to **Sleeps Her Way to the Top** faster than charm from the top (of course). And what better way to fire things up a little than by channeling your inner Don Juan.

Use those quarters you've been saving for the vending machine and instead order some lovely flowers to have sent her way (word to the stupid—you might want to pay cash for those flowers so they can't be traced back to you so easily). Make sure to include a very suggestive message, something along the lines of "I've got my eyes on your bottom line" or "Let's put this matter to bed" or, even better, "Please come to my office and take 'notes.'" After all, it's always more fun if you can see the action yourself. Either way, sign it with the boss's initials (unless of course you think she's already added that notch to her bedpost). After the bombshell confronts him, those roses won't be smelling so sweet.

No Change Given

RISK LEVEL

TARGET: Kisses the Boss's Ass

Office Supplies

Those taken from your victim's desk

An afternoon trip to the vending machine is a norm in almost every office, and we all know what we're going to find: a Snickers bar, a stale bag of trail mix, and the "healthy" pretzels we probably should be getting. This week though it's time to shake things up a little. It's time to give your coworkers a real treat, perhaps a stapler, bobble-head doll, a bag lunch, or a favorite pen or parking pass.

To get this gag to work your first task is to make friends with the guy who refills the vending machine. Do whatever is necessary to win him over. After all, you're an executive.

Once a friendship has formed, fill him in on your plans. The night before his arrival collect as many items from **Kisses the Boss's Ass's** desk as possible. The more personal the better. The next day the two of you can work together to replace those pretzels and Oreos with nameplates, pencil cups and calendars.

Watch the fun as **Kisses the Boss's Ass** starts begging for quarters.

When I Say Jump . . .

RISK LEVEL

TARGET: He Who Knows Everything

Office Supplies

Letterhead

This is a great prank for **He Who Knows Everything**. He's been driving you crazy with tales of perfection . . . his, certainly, not yours. And you're sick of watching him lick **Idiot with All the Power's** shoes, trying to wow everyone with his fabulous work skills. Well, here's the perfect revenge.

Send **He Who Knows Everything** a memo, from **Idiot with All the Power** if possible. If not, anyone with a position of power will do. Your goal is to get Mr. Everything jumping. The memo should inform **He Who Knows Everything** that something very important has come up (your line of work will determine what would be so important) and you're going to need him to put aside all other work until this project is complete. And then you assign the project. The most tedious, ridiculous project you can come up with. Maybe it's counting every individual pen in the supply room or going through the last twenty-five years of accounting records to find a missed payment. Or, maybe it's simply a report on widgets that we all know will take at least three days to compile. Either way, it's going to make everyone else wonder why **He Who Knows Everything** isn't getting the work done that he's supposed to, and it's really going to confuse **Idiot with All the Power** when a widget report lands on his desk instead of the payroll checks he's been waiting for.

Office Alfresco

RISK LEVEL

TARGET: Stick Up Her Butt

Office Supplies

Masking tape

This is a time-intensive trick that should be done at the end of the day when everyone has gone home—everyone, that is, except the fellow pranksters you've convinced to lend a hand.

Move as much of **Stick Up Her Butt's** office furniture and belongings as possible to her parking space outside the building. Try as best you can to arrange them in the same position they appeared in her office. When she drives in to work the next day, she'll get a clear message of where she can "park" it!

Everyone Loves a Nice Potted Plant

RISK LEVEL

TARGET: Stick Up Her Butt

Office Supplies

A potted plant, marijuana seeds, watering can

Now I know you don't smoke pot because you certainly wouldn't have made it to Executive Level unless you were on the straight and narrow. So that's why you're going to need a little help from your friends, so to speak, to pull this prank off. Call up that stoner who lives down the street and ask if you can have any old pot seeds that he might have lying around. Heck, you don't even need a seed, just ask him to hand you an old roach or the remnants from his bong. Collect them in a plastic bag and zippity-doo-dah your way to work.

Grab the watering can and make your rounds. It looks like everyone's plants could use a little drink. Once in **Stick Up Her Butt's** office, secretly slip your pot seeds into her flowers. And wait. This prank is going to take a little time. After all, you actually have to wait for the plant to grow, but it will be well worth the wait when **Idiot with All the Power** suddenly notices strange plants growing in **Stick Up Her Butt's** begonias.

All Glued Down

RISK LEVEL

TARGET: Kisses the Boss's Ass

Office supplies

Desk, super glue

This is an easy prank to execute, but one that could get you in loads of trouble. And that's why it's so great.

All you need is an hour or two and a big bottle of super glue. Then head on over to **Kisses the Boss's Ass's** desk and get to work. Start by super gluing everything down, the pencil cup holder, the pen left sitting on the blotter, his dictionary, and of course the empty soda can. If you're really brave, glue the drawers shut and his mouse down.

Then sit back and watch the confusion as **Kisses the Boss's Ass** struggles to get back to work.

Getting the Boss's Goat

RISK LEVEL

TARGET: Idiot with All the Power

Office Supplies

A goat head, cake box, party supplies, duffle bag or shopping bag, World's Best Boss card, cash

In some countries a goat's head is a delicacy. In ours it is not. But maybe it's time you start introducing more exotic food to your fellow employees, and this is the perfect dish for **Idiot with All the Power**. He's bold, he's brave, and he's your fearless leader. Most importantly, he's everyone's friend and always willing to share a special treat when it comes his way.

For this prank your first stop is going to be the butcher shop, and my guess is that this is something you're going to have to order up ahead of time. My advice: make the order under a false name, pay with cash, and send a friend for pickup. This is a big one, a serious prank, and you don't want anyone tracing it back to you.

Once you've got the head in hand (and keep in mind any head will do, a horse's head did a fantastic job in *The Godfather*), go to your local party store for a beautiful white cake box (big enough to hold a head), some pretty ribbon, napkins, plates, maybe even some balloons to keep things festive, and of course a banner that says "World's Best Boss."

You'll need to get into the office early to make this prank work. Or stay late and let your surprise sit overnight. That's up to you. Either way, you're going to have to come up with a strategic way to sneak your box, head, and other festive supplies in without anyone seeing you. I recommend a duffle bag. Aren't you going away this weekend? Or to the gym?

When no one is around set up your little party in the conference room. Blow up the balloons, hang your banner, lay out your napkins and forks, leave a card addressed to **Idiot with All the Power**, and of course, place the goat head in the cake box and wrap it in pretty ribbons. Obviously **Idiot with All the Power** is going to understand how much his employees love him, and it's

only natural they would want to throw him a party on Boss's Day.

Once setup is complete, leave. Leave the office and don't come back until a number of your co-workers have come in. If you've chosen to go ahead with your little plan in the morning, then it's perfectly natural for you to stroll in like you do every day, coat in hand, ready to work. No one will be the wiser when **Idiot with All the Power's** surprise "cake" is unveiled.

The Office Switcheroo

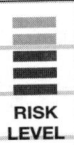

RISK LEVEL

TARGET: Clueless and Hot Temp

Office Supplies

A hand truck, dolly, or other device for moving heavy objects

Clueless is so dumb you sometimes wonder how he gets to his desk in the morning, despite the name plate and map you drew for him on his first day. How does this guy ever make it in the real world? And how could he have possibly gotten himself as far up the ladder as he has?

You're going to need some time for this prank and a lot of help. It's not an easy one, but definitely worth it when all is said and done. The first step is planning a night when your moving crew can stay late, and don't forget to bring some cash. To keep them happy, to keep any movers happy, you're going to be expected to supply them with pizza and a twelve-pack.

Once the office has cleared for the night, it's time to get to work. Your job? To move every piece of furniture, every file and every knick-knack from **Clueless's** office to an empty cube. If you can't find an empty cube and have the manpower and the will, my advice is to move **Hot Temp** from her lowly cube into **Clueless's** office. But just moving boxes isn't going to be enough. Posters need to be hung, pictures arranged on desks, books on shelves, and files back in the cabinet. Your goal is not just to make them think someone moved their crap; it's to make them believe that somehow **Clueless** has been brilliantly demoted and that **Hot Temp** is the new woman in charge. The switcheroo will have them both scratching their heads and you rolling in the aisles.

Fork Lift

RISK LEVEL

TARGET: Everyone in the office

Office Supplies

None

Over the course of several weeks, swipe as many plastic forks as possible from the company cafeteria and conference rooms. Be patient so that you can collect enough to really make an impact. Pretty soon the office manager will be completely baffled by the rise in her plastic utensil budget!

When you're satisfied with your booty, arrive at the office very early one morning. Litter the entire grounds with the forks, sticking them into every patch of grass or dirt you can find. Your landscaping is sure to confuse the entire staff!

A Little Advice for You

TARGET: Talks Too Much

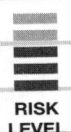

RISK LEVEL

Office Supplies

Computer

There's no doubt that **Talks Too Much** drives everyone insane with her incessant chatter. A conversation with her never lasts fewer than forty-five minutes and in addition to office gossip you're bound to hear all the details of the latest celebrity wedding or breakup. **Talks Too Much** is also never afraid to share all the intimate details of her own relationship with **Clock Watcher**, details that no one wants to know. And that's why this is the perfect prank for her.

While **Talks Too Much** is away from her desk regaling another victim with stories of her boring and not-so-torrid love affair, you can make your move. Slip into her chair and bang out a quick Dear Abby e-mail. What do I mean? Well, you are going to send an e-mail from **Talks Too Much's** computer to everyone in the office asking for advice or opinions on her latest trauma. Could it be that she just found out about an STD and she needs to know how to tell **The Intern**? Or maybe it's that she needs advice on how to handle **Idiot** with **All the Power** and the advances he makes when they're alone in the copier room together? Or, if you're not feeling brave, you could keep it simple and ask for advice on how to handle the strange rash she's discovered on her butt.

Turning the Office on Its Head

TARGET: Idiot with All the Power

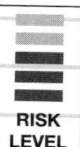

RISK LEVEL

Office Supplies

None

This prank isn't for the faint of heart, or anyone with a heart condition for that matter. It's going to take a lot of hard physical labor and require that you put in a night or even work the weekend.

Your mission? To finally show **Idiot with All the Power** what it's like when his world gets turned upside down. With your trusty team of workers by your side, get into **Idiot with all the Power's** office and turn it around, literally. The desk, the chair, filing cabinets, and every book, every stack, and every pile on his bookshelves—turn it all upside down.

Ready for Signature

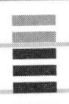

RISK LEVEL

TARGET: Idiot with All the Power

Office Supplies

Computer

The signature line on an e-mail is a prankster's best friend. Almost everyone has one, that official paragraph at the bottom of every e-mail that includes name, company name, address, and contact information. The beauty of a signature line is that no one looks at it again once they've set it up. In other words, no one pays attention to the little things.

This prank is perfect for **Idiot with All the Power.** He's always sending stupid forward e-mails anyway and there's no better way to get him back.

While he's away at one of his long-winded but useless meetings, slip into his chair and change his signature. For the really brave, and those willing to risk more than just a note in the file, change his signature line to something like "This Job Sucks" or "What a Shithole." If you're not quite that brave and not willing to risk it all, you could simply change his name to Stud Muffin or Cool Dude. See how long it takes for him to notice.

Chained to the Job

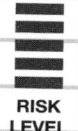

RISK LEVEL

TARGET: Mr. Competitive

Office Supplies

A U-shaped bike lock or bike chain with padlock

At any point during the day sneak out into the parking lot and get yourself to **Mr. Competitive's** ride, ducking between the cars to avoid being seen as much as possible. Once there, simply slip the lock or the chain through the center of the wheel and around the tire. This will be easier on a two-wheeled vehicle with spokes. If **Mr. Competitive** drives a car, you are likely going to have to remove the hubcap to get the chain or lock through. Once you've made the connection, lock it tight and throw away the key.

You have just essentially "booted" **Mr. Competitive,** and there's no way he's going to be able to drive anywhere without doing serious, irreparable damage to his car. His only option, a call to a locksmith or a trip to the hardware store for a chain cutter.

For those who know **Mr. Competitive's** penchant for upholding the law at all costs I would highly suggest wearing gloves at the scene. It's very likely he keeps a fingerprint kit in the car, and the last thing you want is to be printed and booked.

Love in an Elevator

TARGET: Anyone riding the elevator

RISK LEVEL

Office Supplies

An incredibly lewd and disgusting picture, super-sticky tape

The beauty of this prank is that it's office wide. Whoever gets in the elevator is your lucky victim.

Find the most disgusting picture you can. Of course, the web is an obvious source for this, but so is the office copy machine. We've all seen the skits of someone making a copy of their butt. Well, what else could you do? You're an executive now, I think you can come up with some ideas. Whatever you do, make it gross and uncomfortable, certainly not the kind of picture you want to be caught looking at, let alone staring at.

Once you have your picture in hand, head to the elevator during a quiet moment. Maybe right after everyone arrives at work or during a big office meeting. All you need to do is, using as much tape as possible, tape that picture to the inside of the elevator doors. Make sure the tape is sticky enough that it will be almost impossible to remove. That way when the doors close and everyone is facing forward, they'll have something to talk about besides which floor they're on.

You've Been Nailed

RISK LEVEL

TARGET: Anyone with an office at the end of a hallway

Office Supplies

Hammers, nails, screwdrivers, drills, wood, sheetrock, tape, paint

This isn't a prank that will work in just any office. You need to have just the right setup, preferably a hallway or area that sets the executive office suites apart from the rest of the peons (that's you, by the way).

With your gang of trusty pranksters, quietly slip into the office (if that's at all possible with lumber, electric drills, and sheetrock, but you'll figure it out) and begin work. Your job? To wall off the executive suites and make it look believable. At the end of the hall leading to their office build a wall, paint it and set up bookshelves or a desk in front. Make it look like somehow this was planned and meant to be and how they're going to get to their desks will be a mystery to everyone.

Sweat Equity

If you thought some of my other pranks need time, this is really a doozy and one that you're unlikely to finish in just one night. I recommend a Sunday, later afternoon into evening.

While the Cat's Away ...

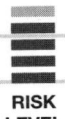

RISK LEVEL

TARGET: Kisses the Boss's Ass

Office Supplies

A mini tape recorder

This is an executive-level prank only because it takes a high level of persuasiveness to get this one to work and very careful execution to avoid being fired.

While the cat's away the mice will play, and there's no better fun than when **Idiot with All the Power** escapes for a long weekend in the country. Before he heads out, convince him that you were reading *Fast Company* magazines and all successful businessmen have their most trusted employees tape record meetings while they're out so they can secretly keep tabs on what's happening and how people are behaving. Remember, he's an idiot, and he'll love your tip. After all, he didn't get to be all-powerful by just following the lowlife crowd.

Once **Kisses the Boss's Ass** sits down to take charge of the meeting, flip that tape recorder on and let loose. This is the time when you want all of your prankster buddies involved. Have **Hot Temp** kindly ask **Kisses the Boss's Ass** to stop touching her like that when he speaks, and have **Talks Too Much** tell **Kisses the Boss's Ass** to put his pants back on. With everyone working together there's no doubt **Idiot** **with All the Power** will have some questions for ~~**Kisses the Boss's Ass**~~ when he returns.

Do I Hear One Dollar?

RISK LEVEL

TARGET: Idiot with All the Power or Mooch

Office Supplies

None

This is a great prank to play on just about anyone. It might cost you your job, but hey, that's the price of brilliance.

Create an online auction account for **Idiot with All the Power** or better yet for **Mooch,** using her office e-mail address for the contact information. Then, go into the office early one morning (yes, we do have to lose sleep to maintain our Executive Pranking status) and take a picture of her computer, her desk chair, and her bookshelf, and then post the objects on the online auction site for sale. She'll receive a notification when the winning bid comes in. Going . . . going . . . gone!

The Incredible Moving Car

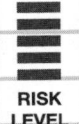

RISK LEVEL

TARGET: Stick Up Her Butt

Office Supplies

The keys to your victim's car

It's hard enough to get someone to loan you a pen in the office, let alone car keys. Of course, to really make this prank work you can't actually ask for the keys, you're going to have to find a way to just get them for a couple of hours.

The minute you do get **Stick Up Her Butt's** keys, head to the local hardware store, have copies made, and slip the keys back in her purse before she notices. Once you have the copies made, you have the keys to a prank that can last you years, or at least as long as **Stick Up Her Butt** stays on the job.

Now, you know **Stick Up Her Butt**, every Wednesday she wears the pink sweater, each morning she stops for a large half-caf nonfat mocha, and each day she parks in the third row, second spot from the end. Isn't it time she lived a little? Pick a day, any day, just make it random and head out to the lot. Move her car three spaces over, no more. A few days later, head out again; now move it a row or two. A week or so later get really brave and try the other side of the lot. A month or so . . . well, you get the picture.

Jell-O, How Are You?

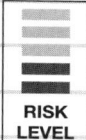

RISK LEVEL

TARGET: Stick Up Her Butt

Office Supplies

Large box of Jell-O, Jell-O mold, stapler

Oh, the wonders of Jell-O. Those fastidious office workers really hate finding their office supplies encased in food products. Of course, **Super Slob** might not even notice. He might even appreciate it if he's hungry enough. So best to stay with a victim a little more responsive to the jiggle. **Stick Up Her Butt** is a good bet.

This trick will require that you stay late one night. (I know! I know!) Make sure your victim has left for the evening before stealthily working your way to his office and making off with his stapler or tape dispenser.

Secrete it away in your messenger bag and take it home with you.

Once at home, prepare the Jell-O package according to package directions. Pour into mold and place stapler in the center. Let set overnight in the fridge. Go into work early, before your victim (which might mean you have to be quite the early bird if you are involving someone like **Stick Up Her Butt**). Remove the stapler from the mold in the target's office and remove all traces of evidence.

A Trifling Good Time

RISK LEVEL

TARGET: Mooch and Old Timer and of course anyone who is hungry

Office Supplies

A strong stomach,
whipped cream,
fresh berries,
2 beets,
1 pound cooked
ground beef,
1 frozen pound cake,
sugar,
lemon juice,
barf bags

You might want to do this one on an empty stomach. Prepare a trifle. Here's a special recipe for you:

Ingredients:

A container of fresh berries

2 grated beets (no need to cook them)

¼ cup cream sherry

1 teaspoon fresh lemon juice

1 tablespoon white sugar

1 loaf pound cake (buy frozen at your supermarket)

1 pound sautéed ground beef

1 can whipped cream

Directions:

1. Combine the beets, sherry, and lemon juice in a bowl. Set aside.
2. Cut the ends off the pound cake. Cut into pieces, each piece about ⅓ of an inch wide.
3. Assemble the trifle by placing a layer of cake slices on the bottom of a fairly shallow glass serving bowl. Spoon half the beet mixture over the cake slices. Cover with ½ the beef mixture. Cover with whipped cream. Repeat, ending with whipped cream topping. Top with a sprinkling of fresh berries for effect. Refrigerate overnight.

Take your masterpiece into the office and leave it in the break room with some paper plates and forks. This one really might be worth setting up your camera beforehand. Watch as **Mooch** and **Old Timer** dig in with abandon. Trifle: Fifteen bucks. The look on their faces as they try not to swallow: Priceless.

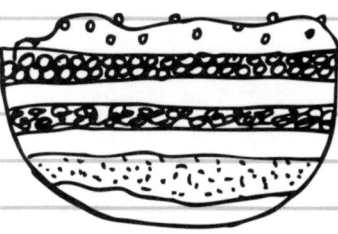

Rock On

RISK LEVEL

TARGET: The entire office and anyone calling the office

Office Supplies

None

This prank could get you in Big Trouble if you do it successfully, and depending on your choice of music.

If your office has hold music for callers, it's very likely the radio or MP3 device is located next to the box that controls the phones. This might take a little sleuthing. But you can do it: You're the **Number One Prankster**! Once you find out exactly where it is, take a quiet moment to change the station or the MP3 files. I recommend a good AM evangelical preacher or a spectacular heavy metal station. If you have some MP3 files to play with, you can always go with some George Carlin or raunchy comedy routine. Make sure you wipe off your fingerprints for this one. You just might piss off some of the big guys. See you on the unemployment line!

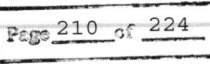

Batter, Batter, Batter, Swing

RISK LEVEL

TARGET: Mr. Competitive

Office Supplies

Computer, iron, a little cash for a trip to the craft store

Make a trip to your local craft store and buy some T-shirts in the company color, along with iron-on paper that's compatible with your computer printer. Go home and print out the company name and/or logo followed by "Softball." Then carefully iron the logos onto the T-shirts.

When you get to work, send out e-mails to **Mr. Competitive**, your co-conspirators, and anyone else you feel like messing with that day. Inform them that **Idiot with All the Power** has asked you to organize a company softball team. Schedule a meeting (or even two) in order to hand out the T-shirts and provide "details" on the league. Let everyone know that the first game will be this Thursday at 4:00. The team will need to be dressed to play and out the door by 3:30.

When the day of the big game arrives, let the softball team know that the boss wants to wish them luck and get a team photo taken with them in his office before they leave. Then stand back and watch as the boss penalizes **Mr. Competitive** for being stupid, and he finds himself sitting on the bench.

Freeze Frame

RISK LEVEL

TARGET: Nervous Nelly and Conspiracy Theorist

Office supplies

A watch

The first course of action is to pick your prey. This one works best on **Nervous Nelly** and **Conspiracy Theorist**. Next, gather as many of your coworkers as possible and persuade them to participate. For optimum impact, convince everyone except your unsuspecting victim to help out.

On the day of the big event, have everyone in your group synchronize their watches as closely as possible. Pick a very specific time for the prank to take place.

When the clock hits, everyone will stop and freeze in place for five minutes. As the victim goes about his daily routine, he'll start to notice his coworkers that are suspended in mid-stride, stooped over the water cooler with an overflowing cup, and taking an eternity to pick up a dropped pen.

The longer everyone can strike the pose, the better your results. **Conspiracy Theorist** may even go running out into the street to see where the mothership has landed!

Take Your "Daughter" to Work

RISK LEVEL

TARGET: He Who Knows Everything

Office Supplies

Some breathmints might help

On Take-Your-Daughter-to-Work Day, bring your main squeeze to work with you. When the opportunity arises, introduce her to **He Who Knows Everything** as "Mandy," the CEO's daughter. Explain that you'll be showing Mandy the ropes all day long.

A little later in the day, have a coworker pass a message from you to **He Who Knows Everything** asking him to stop by and demonstrate his job responsibilities to Mandy. Then, when you know he is just around the corner, commence a really hot makeout session with your girlfriend. **He Who Knows Everything's** eyes will pop right out of his head!

Fast-track

This one works even better if you're a female prankster and you treat the victim to some girl-on-girl action!

Outlining the Crime Scene

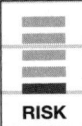

RISK LEVEL

TARGET: Clock Watcher

Office Supplies

Masking tape

This prank is a little elaborate, so be prepared to put in some overtime. Once you're sure that all potential witnesses have gone home, approach **Clock Watcher's** workspace and methodically outline every item on his desk with masking tape. Once you've marked the position of his computer, mousepad, stapler, phone, etc., start removing the stuff and find a new home for it. The copy room may be the perfect spot!

The next day, **Clock Watcher** will feel like he's walking in on a crime scene with the tell-tale "chalk outlines" of his victimized office supplies. See how long it takes him to follow the trail of clues and rescue his belongings from your hiding place.

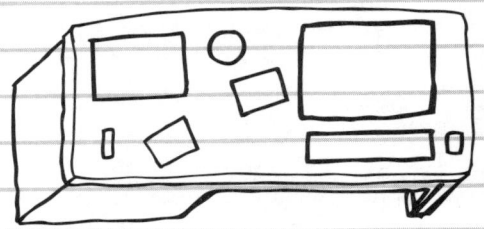

Creating a Lover's Nest

RISK LEVEL

TARGET: Stick Up Her Butt

Office Supplies

*A condom (unused please, people!),
important-looking papers*

Every office has a crazy rumor mill. A lot of the dirt is usually based on fact, but wouldn't it be fun to make the place even more like a soap opera?

When you know the conference room isn't being used, go in and spread the important-looking papers all over the table, letting some of them fall to the floor. Unwrap the condom and make sure to give it that "just used" look—stretch it out with your hands and crumple it up a bit—before strategically placing it on the floor where it's easily seen from the doorway. Be-

fore you leave, turn over a chair for good measure.

When you're finished, swing by **Stick Up Her Butt's** office saying **Idiot with All the Power** was just looking for her and you saw him and **Sleeps Her Way to the Top** heading for the conference room.

The poor innocent will be dumbstruck when she finds her coworkers' love nest!

Trading Spaces

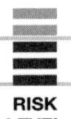

RISK LEVEL

TARGET: Woeful Wallflower and Super Slob

Office Supplies

Digital camera

You've seen them: the offices that have been painstakingly decorated and accessorized to re-semble a home away from home. **Woeful Wallflower** has knick-knacks on every shelf, wall hangings cov-ering every square inch, and even a little welcome mat just inside her door. You just know that she's the one who spurred the memo from HR forbidding office holders to hang wallpaper on company prop-erty. Well, what if **Woeful Wallflower's** "home away from home" were trans-formed into the neighbor-ing work space that looks more like a trailer park?

When most employees have left for the day, gather up your co-conspirators and get ready for the big move. If **Woeful Wallflower** locks her office every night, find a way to place a piece of tape over the door latch to prevent it from closing tightly. It's time for the switcheroo! You can use your digi-tal camera to take photos of both offices first, to make sure you're able to replicate the rooms ex-actly. Move all the stuff from **Woeful Wallflower's** office to **Super Slob's**, being sure to position the objects exactly as they were. Once you're confident that every cat poster is perfectly hung and every dirty coffee cup is precisely placed, you can call it a night.

   Be sure to show up early the next morning to watch the chaos you've wreaked. Poor **Woeful Wallflower**

will be horrified to find her lovely welcome mat replaced with an old hamburger wrapper. **Super Slob** will likely be so confused he'll just turn around and go home!

Snow Job

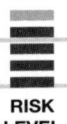

RISK LEVEL

TARGET: Idiot with All the Power

Office Supplies

Phone

Take your buddy from HR out for a nice lunch and hit her up for a favor. Ask her for the number and password to the 1-800 recording for the "Office Closed" message that all employees check on snowy days.

This knowledge is power, my friend. You could play this one any number of ways. If the weather is questionable one morning, program the message (actually you might want to ask a nonwork friend to do the actual recording so it's not easily traced back to you) to say that the office is closed. Then show up to work like a good little employee. You, **Idiot with All the Power,** and your friend from HR—unless you're *really* heartless—will be the only ones to show up that day.

Or if you'd rather pick a day when the office really is closed, program the message to say otherwise. Then all of those poor schmucks will be up before dawn, shoveling out their cars and donning their long underwear, cursing out corporate America all the while . . .

I'll Have Pepperoni on Mine

RISK LEVEL

TARGET: Idiot with All the Power

Office Supplies

Phone, credit card

This prank could set you back a few bucks, but boy will it be worth it!

Let your fingers do the walking and find the number of a stripper service. Tell the booker that you're planning an office bachelor party for your boss and schedule the surprise for about fifteen minutes after the start of your next big company-wide meeting. You might want to tell them that a pizza delivery costume or something similar will work best in order to get her past the receptionist.

Try to contain your excitement as the meeting begins. When the pizza for **Idiot with All the Power** finally arrives, sit back and enjoy the show. Believe me . . . you won't be the only one happy to give the lady your full attention. And all because of you, that meeting will go down in history as the best ever!

Potheads Unite

RISK LEVEL

TARGET: Nervous Nelly

Office Supplies

A lot of paper, computer

Nervous Nelly is a sweet girl, but she hasn't lived life to its fullest. She lived at home while she was in college, never went to a kegger, and refuses to put any toxins in her body. You think it's high time she was exposed to real life!

Use your computer to create a flyer that says:

Print a ton of copies and start posting them everywhere: at clubs, on telephone poles, college hangouts, etc. Pretty soon **Nervous Nelly's** phone will be ringing off the hook with everyone looking for a fix!

MARIJUANA RESEARCH

Test subjects needed to study the side effects of marijuana.

The Bill Clinton Foundation for Better Understanding (or some other made-up clinic or research group)

Contact: **Nervous Nelly** at (insert her phone number)!

That's What She Said

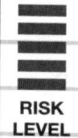

RISK LEVEL

TARGET: The whole office

Office Supplies
Computer, paper, envelopes,
and stamps

Have you ever wondered what's really in those files in HR? Wouldn't you love to know the nitty-gritty of what really goes on behind closed doors? Rumor has it that **Stick Up Her Butt** was once a stripper (or was that **Sleeps Her Way to the Top**?). The truth lies in those files—the files you'll never get into. That is, unless you can pull off this prank.

One night at home, create a very official-looking survey. Use company letterhead if possible and a very sophisticated-looking font. The goal is to create a phony review form reportedly issued by national corporate head-quarters. Introduce the questionnaire to the office with an explanation about how the head office would like to promote an open-door policy with all of its employees, and in that spirit, is asking that everyone answer the questions with complete honesty and candor. Participants will be offered full confidentiality and are guaranteed they will not suffer any repercussions for whatever admissions they make. To ensure that they trust you completely, supply them all with a self-addressed stamped envelope with your new P.O. Box.

When making up your form consider some of the following questions:

- If trapped on a desert island with any one coworker, who would you most like to have there with you and why?
- If you learned that one of your coworkers was facing criminal charges, who would you most likely suspect and why?
- When reading the following words, write down the name of the coworker who first pops into your head and explain why.

1. Idiot
2. Hot
3. Loser
4. Thief
5. Backstabber
6. Slacker

- Has there ever been a time when you've been surprised that someone wasn't fired? Describe the circumstance.
- What's the juiciest office gossip you know?
- What's the stupidest office policy and why is it stupid? Who ignores it?

When you've had a chance to review all the forms (and get a good chuckle, as well as some major blackmail ammunition), "accidentally" share them with your coworkers. What would happen if somehow the file containing all of this private information was revealed? What would happen if it suddenly showed up in e-mail inboxes everywhere or was delivered to the Big Boss Man via interoffice memo?

Undoubtedly, you'll leave the office in complete chaos . . . but they'll make sure you never come back!

Cover Your Ass

Tips For Talking Your Way Out of Anything

- Blame it on the guy you know already has two warnings in his file.
- Tears speak louder than words, especially if you're a dude. Tell some sob story about a terminally ill family member and your mounting debt. Your interrogator will become so uncomfortable he'll just look for a way out of there.
- Shrug and shake your head quizzically.
- Tell them it's all research for a book you're doing on the best companies to work for. You're currently working on the chapter about bosses with a great sense of humor . . .
- Say it was the CEO's idea of a great joke to play on the staff.
- Deny, deny, deny . . .
- Run—and don't look back!

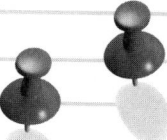

Important Phone Numbers

1-800-FLOWERS

Emergency: 911 (Dude, if you need to look that one up, it's already too late!)

Central Intelligence Agency: 703-482-0623

Department of Homeland Security: 202-282-8000

Federal Bureau of Investigation: 202-324-3000

GM Motor Club: 1-877-466-6867

Headhunters.com: 206-517-0608

Molly Maid: 1-800-MOLLYMAID

National Anger Management Association: 646-485-5116

National Demolition Association: 1-800-541-2412

National Career Development Association: 918-663-7060

National Legal Aid and Defender Association: 202-452-0620

Nationwide Singing Telegram Company: 866-504-TUNE

Orkin Pest Control: 1-800-506-2202

Roto-Rooter: 1-800-GET-ROTO

Staples: 1-800-378-2753

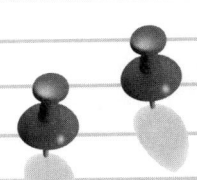

Add your own important numbers here:

_____

_____

_____

_____

_____